To Tame the Hydra

The Hydra, like other creatures, has now evolved the attitudes and attributes needed to survive in its hostile, marshy environment. These, shared among its nine heads, are: rage, ferocity, greed, cruelty, hatred, lust for power, pitilessness, distrust and illusion.

Nevertheless, if it can be domesticated, some of the Hydra's energies could be of value to the community.

Also by Adam Curle

Educational Strategy for Developing Societies, Tavistock, 1963
Planning for Education in Pakistan, Harvard U.P., 1968
Making Peace, Tavistock, 1971
Mystics and Militants, Tavistock, 1972
Education for Liberation, Tavistock, 1973
True Justice, QHS, 1981
In the Middle, Berg, 1986
Recognition of Reality, Hawthorn, 1987
Tools for Transformation, Hawthorn, 1992
The Transforming Force, Carlssons, 1992
Another Way, Jon Carpenter, 1995

To Tame the Hydra

Undermining the culture of violence

Adam Curle

JON CARPENTER

Our books may be ordered from bookshops or (post free in the UK) from
Jon Carpenter Publishing, 2 The Spendlove Centre, Charlbury,
England OX7 3PQ

Please send for our free catalogue

Credit card orders should be phoned or faxed to 01689 870437
or 01608 811969

Our US distributor is Paul and Company, PO Box 442, Concord, MA 01742
(To order, call 201 840 4748)

First published in 1999 by
Jon Carpenter Publishing
2, The Spendlove Centre, Charlbury, Oxfordshire OX7 3PQ
☎ 01608 811969

ISBN 1 897766 51 3

Printed in England by J. W. Arrowsmith Ltd., Bristol.
Cover printed by KMS Litho, Hook Norton

In the last few decades there has been a splendid vanguard, spearhead – I wish there were less of a military word – of women peacemakers on the international scene. I am honoured that some of them have been my friends; for instance Elise Boulding, Scilla Elworthy, Diana Francis, Margareta Ingelstam, Roswitha Jarman, Lynne Jones, Katarina Kruhonja, Mairead Corrigan McGuire, Joanna Santa Barbara, Elizabeth Salter, Christine Soane (sadly now deceased), Vesna Terselic, Betty Williams, Jillian Wychel and indeed others. In addition there are very many more with whom I have not had the privilege of working as closely, or getting to know as well, and many thousands more of course whom I have never met at all. But the collective wisdom, the steadfast courage and the imaginative fire of all these women have put breaks on the juggernaut of war. Their love for humanity, expressed in countless ways as mediators, negotiators, healers, leaders and mothers, has weakened the world's violence and strengthened the culture of peace. For this we owe them a great debt of gratitude which I can only repay, in very small part, by my own work and by dedicating this poor book to them with abiding respect and love.

Adam Curle

Mars asked the planet Earth:
'Who is winning the race?'

'What race?' asked Earth.

'The human race,' said Mars.

'But you can't win the human race,' said Earth.

'No,' said Mars, 'but you could lose it.'

Venus said, 'If you don't interfere,
Perhaps I could help humanity to find itself.'

Contents

A word about myself		1
1	Introduction	3
2	The Hydra	9
3	Such was the world the Hydra made	19
4	Changing the Hydra	31
5	Happiness	37
6	Mind, system and society	51
7	Principle and practice	61
8	Summary	79
9	Strategy for happiness	85
10	Implementation	91
Postscript: A personal message to the reader		95
Notes and bibliography		99
Index		101

Adam Curle

A word about myself

I survived a dreadful conventional schooling, particularly five years at what Thackeray called the Charnelhouse, by playing the flute (mainly Bach), writing poems, and reading the mystics. But university was a delightful, lazy liberation, full of friendship.

I was never much good at passing examinations in regular subjects like physics or history, but better at putting aspects of them together to give a new twist to old disciplines – for example, my interweaving of anthropological and psychological ideas led to my appointment as the first university lecturer in social psychology at Oxford. Or even creating virtually new subjects, such as the mediation of large-scale violence, by adding some elements of psychoanalysis and of Tibetan psychophilosophy. I 'discovered' ways of teaching and of training teachers, of reducing stress, of tackling problems of economic and social development, of dealing with the violence of war. Even in the army (I was a soldier for five years in World War II) my psychological ideas brought me senior rank. Although my more traditional colleagues labelled these subjects as bogus, they got me professorships at reputable places like Harvard.

I wrote books on these topics, but I was essentially an activist, not an academic. For over half my adult life, up to and including today – I am 83 – I have been directly involved in great issues: third world poverty and oppression and, mainly, war. These drew me away from my first, rather too comfortable, chair in England and I never took another university job which did not give me almost complete freedom to put my ideas into practice. The emphasis, first, was on social and educational development.

However, with growing mass violence in many places where I had worked, I was irresistibly drawn into the furnace of war. The first episode, in fact, was resistance to apartheid in South Africa where, (correctly) suspected of conspiracy, I managed to withstand weeks of police interrogation. But from the mid-1960s onward I worked endlessly in a dozen war zones, mainly in Asia and Africa but also Ireland, attempting to disentangle one lethal imbroglio after another. My latest involvement has been in the Balkans, trying for six years to help people to survive the violent chaos with dignity and purpose.

It has been a life of difficult journeys in rickety planes landing on roadways, strange encounters, peril and confusion, bizarre episodes such as guarding unarmed a president against expected assassination, difficult negotiations with dangerous men, loyalty and corruption, the horror of mass graves in Vukovar and Rwanda, wonderful friendships. This book, however, is not concerned with what are only incidentals to the underlying and implacable purpose: which is to stop people torturing and killing each other.

I have had a reasonably successful professional career with chairs, a few honorary degrees and membership of learned societies, but have always been something of an academic outsider. Because much of my peace work has been confidential, I have never sought publicity. I still write poetry, some of which is in this book as a form of 'illustration', but my flute was destroyed by a bomb. I am a semi-lapsed Quaker and a devotee of the Dalai Lama. I have been blamed for not sticking at the same thing, but maintain that life is movement and stasis is death: I never know when engaged in one task what the next one will be. I am still wondering about this; my only true certainty being my loved and loving family.

A.C.

1

Introduction

Friends who know some of my earlier writings, feel that the approach taken in this book may be too unorthodox. But so it should be. The world has changed enormously since I started in the mid-1960s recording my experiences of peace and conflict; and the process has accelerated greatly in the last dozen years. The colonial imperia have disappeared; the bloc of the USSR and its satellites has disintegrated (with a second instalment now perhaps occurring in Russia); a number of other countries are in violent turmoil, including the many new ones; the gap between rich and poor between and within nations is widening; patterns of human life and relationships are vastly changed by the technological revolution; there is a virtually global free market highly susceptible to destabilising manipulation.

These conditions, with their often confusing and convulsive economic, political and psychological corollaries, have generated disorderly and destructive forces which we lack the skill or experience to control. The Great Lakes area of Africa, Bosnia, Somalia, the Caucasus (where my friend Roswitha Jarman has worked courageously and predicts further large-scale violence) are a few of the many places where well-intentioned international bodies have proved sorely inadequate. But this is a new world; it is clearly necessary to abandon earlier concepts, and old methods of dealing with violent conflict, and to work towards devising fresh ones more appropriate to the present. Above all we must learn to replace our current remedies, which have not prevented cruelty and economic chaos, but often increased them. More than any other aspect of the world's turbulence, the financial blizzard from the formerly respected Tiger Economies is the most likely to have a direct impact on Western Europe.

I am not an economist and shall not presume to consider specific economic measures. My concern is the larger formative context out of which this particular issue has grown, along with others affecting life in our world. Unless this is understood and responded to, we will hardly be able to ride out the storm which could strike us. It is not enough to identify and act upon what seems to be the appropriate balance of a free market with a managed or 'social' market that is concerned, at least to some extent, with human well-being. A more fundamental readjustment of our view of society and of ourselves is demanded.

The aim of this short book is to suggest approaches towards new ways of understanding and tackling the planet's surge of violence and confusion.

Physical violence

Those of us who were concerned with the study of violence and the practice of peace-making from approximately 1965 to 1985 worked to develop principles around the concept of *conflict.* We were involved with the analysis of hostile relationships (usually between two parties, groups, nations, etc.) and with developing ways of changing them for the better. We referred to the improvement of these relations as resolution, management, mitigation, transformation, and so on, of conflict, but these were differences mainly of name.

However, since the end of the Cold War we have faced more and more bloody and chaotic situations in which the ruptured relationship is caused less by some relatively local quarrel than by the matrix of impinging external factors. These are the interacting and increasingly worldwide forces of political, economic and military power which are upheld by elements of the elites of virtually every country in the world and contribute a tithe of violence to its culture.

The horrors suffered and inflicted during the Janatha Vimukti Peramuna insurrection and the interminable war between Tamils and Singhalese in Sri Lanka, the ghastly birth pangs of Zimbabwe, the inability of Hindus and Muslims to live together peacefully in the sub-continent of India, the holocaust in Rwanda coupled with the rash of wars covering much of Africa, the intractable (until now, we hope) troubles in Northern Ireland, 'Biafran' starvation, the miseries of Tibet, the destruction of the charming and artistic Chakmas, and the wars in former Yugoslavia – these changed my perspective.

I was involved in all of these to some extent, most recently with former Yugoslavia for seven years, while friends and colleagues have reported on comparably discouraging experiences in the Caucasus, Afghanistan, Cambodia, Guatemala, Colombia, Sierra Leone, Somalia, Ethiopia, Liberia, and the whole of the Great Lakes region of Africa – let alone less conspicuous but shameful inequalities and injustices in most of the richer nations. Many of the innumerable armed struggles, for example in Uganda, seem to have been pointless, carried on by habit or reflex rather than purpose. Often, as in Bosnia and Rwanda, there has been a genocidal setting of peoples, rather than regimes, against each other.

And other sorts of misery were added to the pains of the world.

Statehood was growing weaker but often cruel and more tyrannical; gulfs between rich and poor were growing wider, both between and within nations; warlords were taking the place of statesmen; at the local and national levels desperate crimes of violence increased; the health of the environment was increasingly jeopardised and no political leader powerful enough to retard the deterioration was brave enough to do so; great transnational corporations, unaccountable save to their shareholders, had an increasing control over global markets; individual speculators acquired the ability to shake the world; everywhere it was the rich who had the power – they called, so to speak, the shots and in some places had little hesitation in shooting, literally or metaphorically, if their interests were challenged.

However, the chief characteristic of this emerging world is, I began to see, the interconnectedness of the destructive forces, the interwoven and increasingly interacting worldwide forces of economic, political and military power: a *global culture of violence*. This is fuelled at all levels, from individual to nation and perhaps even to international bloc, by the hope for power and profit. The greater the hope, the more urgent the craving. And the hope is intensified by a wealth of evidence showing amazing and unprecedented possibilities. By the same token, the fear of *not* gaining the advantages, or the dread of losing them, aggravates despairing anger. These are explosive feelings.

This situation, I believe, requires a shift in our ideas of peace. There will, of course, always be a need for peace-making methods of mediation, negotiation, reconciliation and the like. We also need, however, to understand and learn to *withstand* and to *transform* within ourselves and our own societies the attitudes and activities out of which the culture of violence develops.

Without progress in this sphere, work on any specific conflict will be of little, except perhaps temporary, avail.

In attempting to examine these crucial issues, which already affect our daily lives through their economic impact, I have found myself exploring paths which may seem strange or irrelevant. These include the Hydra, the term I use to describe the interdependency of forces that dominate our world; the often deluded quest for happiness and its effect on peace or violence; the extension of mind beyond the individual; the lessons to be learned from systems theory, psychology and neuroscience.

If these explorations have lured me far from my conventional path, they have also taken me back to it – but I believe closer to the end of my journey of exploration.

A note on presentation

Before starting a detailed examination of the Hydra, happiness, the extended mind and the other topics with which these pages are concerned, I should say something about the way in which I have tried to present them, and particularly their impact on our ways of thought, our attitudes, our feelings. But how can we grasp the enormities of despair and misery, the terror, horror and confusion brought to such a large proportion of humanity by the last eighty-five or so years of cruelty, social convulsion and rape of the environment? Facts and figures are not much help; sometimes they only stand between us and the true sense of things – and in any case someone will point out that they are inaccurate and so dismiss the whole argument; but what difference does it make anyway to know precisely how many millions were killed in any particular war, or died in any particular famine or epidemic?

It is the feelings that are evoked by these appalling happenings that shape the future; if we cannot *sense* them, we can do little to affect it.

In fact the art of Goya, or Picasso's Guernica tell us far more than the statistics of war. I have often felt frustrated by the failure of the type of writing expected from an academic to convey the *full reality* of a place or a situation, but have occasionally tried to do so through poetry. In the attempt to add some of this other dimension to our exploration, I have included some in these pages.

Our all is nothing, our nothing's everything.
Todo y nada.
The things we tell are no things,
Whispers of dead grass, silent sighing of wind.
Our circling thoughts are void,
the voidness of mere absence.
Our ears echo with silence,
Our eyes reflect emptiness,
Our lips brush only space.
The skin we stroke is made of stars
that fly apart a million miles a second.
We are everywhere and nowhere,
The no things that are all things.

We try to find the way
between the illusions
and a reality too awesome
for acknowledgement,
the narrow middle way
between life and death,
the first too bright,
the second unfashionable;
between the crem and the high altar
an aisle of oblivion,
so let's leap on the hearse
for the magical mystery tour
that always,
whatever the expected destination,
leads to the same place.
Narrow, dark and lonely.
Todo y nada.

The young commander, exhausted and exultant,
sprawled on his seat and reported his apparent
triumph; the enormous convoy
was suffering slow piecemeal destruction
trapped on the long causeway; no escape,
exploding ammo trucks blocking front and rear
while sodden jungle lapped on either side.

He thought, in his tired high, he'd won the war.
Ah, but he hadn't. No one ever does.
The so-called victors will become aware,
though trying to ignore the evidence,
their fight for justice or for liberation
(let alone a less high-sounding cause)
by some grim logic spawns the opposite;
prison walls make dark the land, the vultures
flop gorged around the slaughter houses,
at dawn the secret police still make their calls,
the myriad mourners are uncomforted,
there's something precious everyone has lost.

And soon the knives of war are honed again.

2

The Hydra

This creature, it will be recalled, was a vast many-headed water snake which Hercules must kill to fulfil his Labours. But as soon as one head was cut off, another grew in its place. Hercules overcame this difficulty by getting his companion to cauterise the stump immediately after the decapitation. I should explain that I use the term because so frequently in these days, the apparent solution to a problem is followed by the re-emergence of a comparable matter: the war in Bosnia was, in a fashion, brought to an end, but another starts in nearby Kosovo; the United States legislated against the sale of alcohol, but subsequent criminal activity to break Prohibition on a huge scale soon created worse social problems than drinking. I shall not, however, consider ways of 'killing' our Hydras because, as will be explained, virtually all of us share something of the Hydra spirit – to slay it would in a sense be suicide. I use the term to mean a destructive and/or violent practice or activity essentially arising out of a greedy desire for gain; one reason for its ineradicability is its usual linkage with others comparable.

The Hydra is largely a product of globalisation. This is a contemporary buzz word, but of course the condition is very far from new. It means that things such as climatic change spread or have a knock-on effect throughout the world. Of course we use the word also to describe human contacts or activities, but until the recent advent of jet travel and electronic mail, the repercussions of an event in China or India took weeks to impact Europe. Now it is almost instantaneous. Globalisation is sometimes thought to imply homogenisation, but of course this is not necessarily the case; the advent of cinema and of Christianity, for example, did not have the same effects!

Globalisation also has its champions, those who maintain that one cannot have too much of a good thing, whether it is trade, or technology, or a particular economic, cultural or political principle. And its enemies; those who believe that some principle or activity is undesirable or even destructive, and therefore the more restricted the better; or perhaps that some things are desirable in a particular limited context but become toxic, as do some substances, if opened up and widespread. Herein is ample scope for controversy. My hopes and fears concerning globalisation will probably become clear as this book proceeds.

One thing we can be certain of now, however, is that there are always *some* effects of every event. The crucial element of globalisation is that *every single one* of the myriad human activities that are constantly occurring has some impact upon many others. Moreover each of these impacts has effects intrinsically as unpredictable in complete detail as Heisenberg discovered and stated in his famous theorem. As I write, shortly before Christmas, 1998, we are asking ourselves: What will Clinton – Blair – Congress – above all Saddam Hussein – actually *do*? But we can do no more than make educated guesses.

At this moment, and indeed at very many others in my long life, there have been a great number of factors – military, economic, revolutionary, intellectual – ready to make, or already making an impact on life around me. Some of these are what I term Hydras, that is to say those whose impact is violent or will generate violence. One of these that we are now experiencing is an element in what we admiringly called the Tiger Economies. Its potential has now been revealed in the disruption, if not destruction, of those economies and the chaotic violence generated thereby. We have to consider, however, whether the Hydra's violence had not lain concealed for years: the tens of thousands of workers living in miserable poverty under conditions of oppression and injustice.

Finally we should recognise that the local culture, so to say, of the various heads of the Hydra may differ greatly. They may oppose each other on specific matters relating to territory, resources or ethnicity, or rival each other in their bids for power. But now they virtually all stand for the same sort of world view: That the *Pursuit and Protection of Profit* is the supreme objective, and that it is legitimate to maintain it with violence. They may, of course, conflict with rivals who share their general philosophy, but their real enemies are those who believe that the *Well-being of People* matters more than profit. To those whose value is *PPP*, this is the most obscene antithesis of all, the evil Communists contrasted with the good Conservatives. (Paradoxically, however, the Communist *W-bP* of Europe and China ended more like extreme Conservatives, leaving democracy to the compromising liberals.)

The basic character of the modern Hydra can perhaps best be illustrated by an earlier and much simpler version: the European slave trade.

The slave ships would sail from Europe with goods for sale in West Africa. There they would take on cargoes of slaves captured by the African rulers. These would be carried across the Atlantic, returning laden with goods for the European market – cotton, rum, sugar, etc. This trade of course engendered a great network of economic and indeed social relationships involving, for example, the ship-building industry and the production, sale and distribution of the goods involved – and of course the structure of African and American and Caribbean society. The long-term impact of this triangular trade has been tremendous.

The trade was maintained because it was to the economic advantage of everyone (except of course the unfortunate slaves). But though the merchants and traders shared the same interest in profit, they also competed financially, and at times fought each other at sea. Then as now such adventurers were respected by their own peoples: the piratical slaver Hawkins was honoured by England with a knighthood and the rank of admiral. But indeed that slave trade, like today's Hydra, generated conflict – political in England and, eventually, in America through the terrible Civil War.

The contemporary Hydra differs from the slave trade mainly by being global. The interconnectedness (including the rivalries) of the more powerful nation states; the great unaccountable transnational corporations; at times the vast political blocs (mainly the USA and formerly the USSR), backed where deemed necessary and possible, by military force; the international economic agencies (the World Bank and the International Monetary Fund); all these have imposed their will on the weaker ones. This has not, of course, always been an identical will except in their philosophy of profit. This it is now fashionable to call *growth*, or particularly when applied to the poorer areas, *development*. Let us, however, be honest; the debts incurred in the quest of development have created unfathomable poverty for its victims. This could be disguised as altruism, and indeed is thought to be so by the determined donors of aid. I refer of course to the practice of structural adjustment enforced by the IMF on nations in economic difficulties, but adopted by New Zealand in an extreme form; this appallingly unsuccessful experiment in the 1980s brought nearly a fifth of the population under the poverty line within a few years.

The size and intricacy of the Hydra make it almost impossible to understand exactly how its elements relate to one another or contribute to particular situations of violence or oppression, famine or revolution. It is frequently a concatenation of forces, some present, some generated in the past, impinging, often indirectly, on a particular issue or area.

Take, for example, such contemporary trouble spots as the Gulf or the Balkans. Iraq is still being bombed and its children are dying as a result of punitive but politically completely ineffective sanctions – the oil interests of the G7P* being paramount. Bosnia is more or less at peace, but Kosovo is in flames. Why? The Hydra is little changed. Still persisting are the old fears and antipathies; the dream of a Greater Serbia; the devious and reclusive rule of Milosevic; the West European contemptuous ignorance of Balkan affairs and culture; the humiliating exclusion of Russia from involvement with policy over Kosovo; European (especially British) servility towards America; the American combination of indifference to the outside world with the ruthless use of power against it if feeling menaced; the interests, overt and covert, political and economic, of all parties; and now the suspicious concern of China for the wider world scene. These factors have combined to create a violent situation that could become much worse.

Circumstances vary, but it is clear that generative forces are usually not eliminated by what may seem the end of any particular episode; a fresh head grows, a new conflict breaks out, or perhaps a famine that could lead to new violence. In some areas the interweaving of forces, carried over from earlier situations or more recent happenings, make lasting peace seem a faint hope; the Great Lakes area of Africa is also very obviously such a place.

A related characteristic of the Hydra is that its pattern of action is impermanent. It is subject to frequent unforeseeable events such as natural disasters, climatic irregularity, changes of regime or the deaths of key actors. All of these add to the difficulties of prediction or control. And who indeed can control the controllers, who also are subject to comparable forces?

There is much talk of the globalisation of this or that. What is really most dangerous for the stability and survival of ordered civil society is the globalisation of the Hydra. Its countless interacting ramifications have generated rampant forces that can seldom be predicted and guarded against. A simple and relatively harmless manifestation of this is the constant uncertainty of the economy as it affects our daily lives.

---

* The G7 Plus (G7P) countries include those who are rich but not members of the club, as well as their associates and representatives in poorer ones.

Development of the Hydra

I had a small glass tank filled
with creatures from the local pond.
Once I watched a dragonfly larva
gnawing a tiny fish,
still alive and gasping.

So intense its ravenous
preoccupation, it was
unaware of being also
eaten, at its tail end,
by a water scorpion.

No doubt the Hydra principle is very old, much more so than the African slave trade which I used as a convenient example of a simple form. It is possible, however, that in neolithic Europe a less denominational culture prevailed, as indeed it yet does in remote areas. One example of such a delightful culture still prevailed in the early 1960s among the Chakmas of the Chittagong Hill Tracts, a charming, cheerful and highly artistic Buddhist people. It is one of the many such tragedies of our century that their society was virtually erased by the greed and fire power of Bangladesh. I mourn them.

However, it is perhaps reasonable to suggest that the modern variant of the Hydra began to take shape in Europe around the end of the Middle Ages. During this period rulers tired of the ramshackle constitutions of their fiefdoms and started to build embryonic nation states. This demanded a certain degree of centralisation. A king, for example, found it irksome to have to borrow from his nobles their archers and foot soldiers – who might go home for harvesting! – if he wanted to fight a neighbour. So he set up his own army. This required some central administration and a centralised treasury for military expenditure. This was one factor which stimulated the development of banking, so the great new banks, such as Fugger and the Banco Giro, emerged at this stage. This enhanced the status of the armies, stimulated military and indeed general technology and, some time later, science. The whole interwoven enterprise was given a further boost of legitimacy from the unexpected quarter of Geneva. The teachings of Calvin, though perhaps incorrectly interpreted, suggested that the acquisition of wealth and the raising of social status showed that one was chosen by God to join him in heaven – behaviour was irrelevant; God made the selection for his own reasons and then showered his elect with good things in this world until they joined him in the next. This too, of course, was to the advantage of the banks (formerly handicapped by restrictions on usury) as well as providing funds for the development of new industry and the running of the state.

The growth of this initially simple form of capitalism naturally offered an infinite number of openings for the conditional happiness drive, both rational and ignorant, in particular legitimising the latter. (Conditional happiness is happiness that depends on circumstances rather than our inner state; see Chapter 4 for more detailed definitions).

Gradually the state apparatus emerged. It comprised the military, the financial institutions, science and technology together with industry and relevant teaching and training bodies, and finally, in many countries, a highly attractive (to the entrepreneur) religious teaching. These came together to constitute a system of interaction, official and unofficial, which has lasted, with of course countless additions and refinements, until now. During the twentieth century, particularly the last fifty years, the tempo of technical and hence social change has increased year by year – even day by day.

Hydra components

We may summarise some of the more obvious forces through which the contemporary Hydra may manifest:

Some functions of economic institutions, such as the Multinational Agreement on Investment which if fully implemented may provide for the regulation of governments by the great international corporations; and by these corporations separately and collectively.

The policies of governments with regard to economic growth and having decisive implications for the inequalities of nations and of peoples within those nations.

The military force that governments (sometimes under the guise of the United Nations or NATO) can muster and employ to impose their policies.

The great banks which gain a measure of control nationally and internationally through making loans at rates of interest ruinous to their creditors. In general, the manipulation of market forces to the private advantage of financial institutions or even by individuals.

The arms trade by which governments protect and promote these policies even at the expense of mutual hostility.

The threat of military force.

The G7 officially and probably most of the G7Plus (the other wealthy countries) which, with a few exceptions, are in general agreement on many issues – hoping to affect them to their own interests.

The media, which the rich can acquire and use to their own advantage.

The culture of violence and profit which sanctions and promotes many of these activities.

Above all, the millions of individuals who accept without understanding, tolerate, profit from and/or promote the various specifics of the situation.

These components of the Hydra (and others could be multiplied and subdivided, with many further details added to all) constitute an overarching interdependency. It is in fact a worldwide self-created but largely unplanned system, although some aspects of it, such as military ones like NATO or economic ones like the OECD, are organised differently. Very few of the several areas or factors mentioned above *could exist as they do without most of the others*. If one of them were to be excised, the pressure of the interdependency would fill the vacuum.

The heads of the Hydra – the corporations, the governments, the banks, etc. – may sometimes quarrel, sometimes compete, but in general they need each other if they are to continue functioning in such a way as to achieve their collective goals of control and profit. It is generally felt, for example, that it is to the advantage of the rest of the world that Russia, though often seen as an obstacle to peace, should be kept more or less orderly and prosperous. There may have to be adjustments, but only ones compatible with these long-term shared objectives.

Operation of contemporary Hydras

To conclude this group of arguments, I shall try to sketch the interaction of these Hydra heads – now infinitely more complex than the slave trade – in the faltering world of today.

The interacting pattern of the factors we have been discussing naturally varies from place to place and year to year. Here is one of the dominant examples involving, as is very usual, one or several of the poorer recently independent nations:

Its machinery of state is very flimsy. It is a variant, but a recently changed and largely discarded version of that of the former colonial power; corrupt officials take advantage of the lack of control. The armed forces are still associated with the colonial rule; many of the senior officers, having been trained overseas, feel impelled to take over. The defence budget soars, partly because the arms-manufacturing former colonial power encourages them to purchase its wares, partly because they see a fine chance of advancement, partly out of a genuine aim to preserve internal security, partly because they are afraid of aggression from neighbouring states equally suffering the same traumas of instability, poverty and corruption.

The ex-colonial power may have some vestigial sense of responsibility, but it and its traders, and subsequently the great growing transnational corporations, sense the chance of rich profits. They arrange new deals for raw materials – minerals, timber, rubber, coffee, tea – taking advantage of, and indeed necessitating, ruinously underpaid local labour. These deals are grossly disadvantageous to the poor nations, but they cannot do without them – and indeed the officials who arrange them and act as agents for the rich (whether the colonial powers or the IMF) do very well from them.

But the demands of the armed forces, let alone those for health services, education, and for some display of national splendour such as a new capital free of the imperial trappings of the past, cannot be denied. The banks of Europe and America are only too keen to oblige and an enormous debt is built up. The poor become poorer and before long tribal, linguistic or religious differences flare into violence. The aid which should have enabled them to live a better life is swallowed up in fruitless attempts to pay for the guns and architectural pomp – and, of course, repayment of the debt and the interest on it.

In the Cold War days these local tensions were used by the super-powers to exploit their strategies for global hegemony. The countries of Africa, Asia and Latin America became the proxy battlefields (politically and/or militarily) of the Russian and American Empires. Terrible wars broke out and many who had little to do with the issues at stake (often locally insignificant) were sucked into the flames. War further impoverished the poorest. The international financial agencies, trying to help the poor by the standards of the rich, often made things worse. The rapacious global corporations, trying to promote and protect their interests, scavenged the failing economies regardless of the needs of the people.

The wars spread pollution and did great damage to agricultural potential. Famine became endemic in previously fertile areas and of course illness flourished. Medical and other humane services, reinforced though they were by foreign volunteers, could not keep up with the needs of the sick, of the victims of battle, debt and landmines. Societies were diverted from order, civility and normal human concerns by fear, misery and desperation. Abnormal bigotries and passions arose in this tainted atmosphere; men turned to violence like flowers to the sun. People killed each other for no reason in senseless wars – there was never any problem about obtaining weapons; armed forces around the world, especially in the more indigent areas, rushed to buy more, and more sophisticated, weapons – and to incur more and more debt.

Suspicion, anger, and the rule of tyrants fearful of dissent escalate the use of torture. Ingenious and revolting instruments, purveyed by the same skilled sources that supply the arms, are routinely used by nations which have blithely signed conventions against cruel and unnatural punishment. The culture of violence has developed a subculture of torture.

Because of the turmoil, the land laid waste by war, the ill-planned development schemes of the international agencies; because of the global strategies of the US; because of the overwhelming burden of debt; because of perceptions distorted by suffering and confusion, great shortages developed – a further source of misery and conflict, another situation to be exploited and abused by the vulturine, who seek any profit or advantage, however shameful.

This lethal tangle of inextricably interacting forces is the Hydra. Or rather, it is one aspect of the Hydra: it is that of the slaves, the world's poor, whether American or African.

Turn it upside down, and we see the other side: ourselves, the world's rich, whether African or American. It is we, with our power and craving for profit, who have created this crazed monster that is also attacking us. It has driven us to slaughter each other – and infinitely many others in two world wars; it threatens us with the dreadful weapons we made to protect ourselves; and it drives us into self-centred global turpitude. Finally, in its endless opportunities for growth and extravagance it destroys itself by overheating and corruption, thus endangering the whole structure of what we consider our well-being. Our only course to avoid moral and physical destruction is to tame the monster; at least to try.

The anticipated dread.
You hope it won't come true,
but know it will,
the midnight knock,
the heavy hand upon the shoulder,
curt command, 'Get up'.
Struggling bemused from nightmare
into unreal reality.
Dress slowly, gaining time
to clear the mind
of sick confusion;
have to be alert
or they'll catch you out
and rip your lies apart.
Now the cycle starts;
interrogation,
the tormentor's threat:
'We know how to make you talk,
they always do, your sort,
so save yourself, and us, the sweat;
just answer what we ask,
then you can go'.
Fear wriggles, pleading,
'Why not some trivial facts,
nothing to hurt our side, of course,
but they may really feel
that's all we know.'

Oh no, that's not the way.
They quickly crack you open wide
if you once start to give.
So, just get lost, faint-hearted hope;
play their own game instead,
mislead and confuse them,
taunt and expose their antics
And if they kill you afterwards,
so what? Your pride is saved.

3

Such was the world the Hydra made

The strength of the Hydra

We may ask how it is that the Hydra can exercise such power when we have a magnificent international organisation with specialised agencies to cover almost every possible human contingency. We would no doubt be infinitely worse off without it, but nevertheless the violence goes on unabated – indeed increasing. (It is fashionable, especially in the USA, to deride the United Nations Organisation, but its principal flaw is that the nations are *not* sufficiently united. I have however seen the UN in operation all over the world and am profoundly impressed by the dedication, courage and high calibre of the women and men who serve it.)

But the UN and other international and national bodies are very much at the mercy of the Hydra's interacting components. Its prevailing attitude is dominated by the crude and untempered market; its culture accepts violence as a legitimate means of safeguarding material advantage; it is a system whose life-blood is material gain, but the blood also contains corpuscles of fear for losing the precious gain, and of the illusion that it will bring stable happiness (this is discussed in Chapter 4). How is it possible to control a mind-set that is focused in these ignorant and uncomprehending ways upon the market?

If we want to take any practical action against the Hydra from within, we must among other things psychologically assail the quasi-religious attitudes towards profit that support its destructive outcomes of inequality and war. But to do this, we have to recognise that the present situation is something *we all have collectively created and are too much embroiled with to query with great objectivity*. I cannot stress strongly enough that it could not have come into existence without unwitting and/or passive collaboration – plus, of course the purposeful activity – of a vast number of human beings. A great proportion of these are living or have lived in this century, and although many of the trends were set in previous ages, much of the responsibility is ours. We have to realise that we are the main part of the problem before we can do anything to solve it.

There are other psychological obstacles against understanding the Hydra. One is that we tend to shy away from recognising such complexities, adopting oversimplifications that are in fact distortions of reality intended to make life more manageable. We use the simplifying device of forcing ideas, objects, concepts, into categories. We put them into cages which we call, for example, politics, philosophy, mind, body, good, and evil. This worked fairly well when life was simpler, or rather I should say, when life was *presented* to us more simply. Now that we have enormously more information, much of it presented to us almost simultaneously, some of the simplifications are recognised as inaccurate expressions of reality. So we enlarge the cages into composites such as social psychology, biochemistry, ecology, peace studies and so on. We may combine aspects of what were previously considered quite separate, such as the mental and the physical, and in so doing radically change our perception of them both. But this is seldom enough.

Our simplifications have misled us to envisage a world of discrete things and events – you, me, war, peace, pleasant, unpleasant. We are, however, beginning to realise that it can be seen, as some with vision have always seen it, very differently: as an enormous unity in which countless elements are in constant interaction, merging and separating, changing in shape and function, disappearing and re-emerging in different forms. The concept of a personal God seems to me inconceivable in such a world – yet, paradoxically, I find it easy to believe in a sort of universal holiness; I see cruelty and violence as the fruit of misunderstanding, of illusion, of fanaticism based on oversimplification rather than some rogue gene.

Even so, we are far from recognising fully the profoundly significant fact that everything, even our most trivial action, happens because other things are also happening; and that none of those things would happen as they do, without this interdependence.

When we do gain this understanding, we shall know enough about the Hydra forces to take effective action against them. Until then the stereotyped methods of conflict resolution, or development planning, or whatever term or technique we employ to solve whatever problem, will be of only limited use.

But if we abandon what we are used to, how do we act in a situation of chaos and anarchy? In the past we employed such methods as mediation (which I have practised and written books about), or what has been called by various names such as conflict resolution, transformation, or management. But these, though certainly not unuseful, only affect a specific situation at a particular transient moment of history. What is really needed, however, is to build a solid block of peace and understanding together with the happiness that accompanies and helps to create these states. This block's aim is somehow to effect a *change of heart or awareness or culture*, primarily in oneself as well as many others, and not only in the immediate neighbourhood. (Such a development is discussed later in the section about the Osijek peace group.) Conventional contemporary practice is full of rules and principles, which take the place of *Being*; this needs to be changed. *Mind* must be emphasised, rather than techniques.

Summing up these paragraphs, let me say that the Hydra is not just about violent *phenomena* – war, political oppression, economic violence, and any other orchestrated actions which cause human suffering. These are the expressions of the Hydra, not its essence. The essence is the *underlying spirit*, compounded of greed, ignorance, fear, and the misdirected 'pursuit of happiness'. (The implications of the last phrase and of other references to happiness are discussed at length in Chapter 4.)

Opposition to the Hydra obviously cannot mean killing it, as Hercules did, because a high proportion of humankind is caught in the snares of its multiple systems, actively or passively. It means taming, transforming it. But into what? It would be ludicrous for me to draw up a blueprint for global development. However, it may be possible to delineate the general shape of a transformed Hydra (it will still exist because the system of interconnectedness, though no doubt modified, will continue and be essential – all things, 'good' or 'bad', are connected and interacting). The transformation would be from inequality to justice, from violence to calm, from hatred to love.

How we might work towards this transformation will be discussed later. In the meantime there is more to be said about the growth of the Hydra with its resultant alienating impact and its widening of the gap between rich and poor. Both of course are conducive to tension and direct or indirect violence.

Effects of rapid social change

The rest of this chapter is concerned less with the character and composition of the Hydra, than with its impact on society and the feelings of those affected by it.

These, however, play a significant part in its domination.

The lives of those born around the time of the first world war have in most respects experienced greater changes than have otherwise occurred in the last four hundred.

Technically these have been enormous, covering almost every aspect of life. My early childhood was passed in a house having no running water, electricity, gas, central heating, refrigerator, telephone, car, radio or TV and obviously no fax or e-mail – without which my granddaughters find it hard to communicate (as I now do also). I was bathed in a tub in the kitchen. But the house was large and beautiful; there was room for many guests. Outside were lovely lawns, trees and a pond and a walled kitchen garden – as well as a gardener. There were also two young village women to cook and clean.

Now my wife and I live in a small semi-detached house in London. There is no room for all the grandchildren and we rely on kind neighbours to put them up. There are no servants and we do all the housework and gardening – but with the help of countless electrical gadgets.

In my childhood we travelled long distances by sea rather than by air; even after the war my wife took a month to come by boat from New Zealand. For shorter distances we used the train, but to go as far as Spain was considered wild and adventurous.

When sick we were given barbarously foul-tasting medicines such as gregory powder; the tongue was very important diagnostically; we entirely lacked the 'wonder drugs' such as antibiotics without which I would long since have died. Those, coupled with the jet engine, the silicon chip, electronic communication and contraceptives, have physically, intellectually and morally transformed the simple life in which I grew up.

These changes are, in themselves, unimportant. What matters is their impact on the structure of human relations. Consider, for example, how the supremacy of the motor car has created not just a different way of life for many, but a galaxy of new jobs and professions, and social structures; and of course destroyed a host of others to do with horses. And consider how the development of new technologies has ruined or transformed other ways of life, such as mining and farming, and the communities in which they were carried out.

Collectively these tremendous social and technical shifts have had an equally powerful impact on our values. When as a very young man before the start of the second world war, I wandered around among nomads and peasant peoples in the Arctic and Middle East, I found that the individuals they most admired were not the prosperous merchant nor the landlord. These they might envy, but probably also hated. The ones they respected might, indeed, be very poor, but were known for their generosity, their craftsmanship, their piety, their knowledge of tribal lore, their skill in story telling. Now, when I visit comparable places, I find a great reversal – the rapacious merchant and the oppressive landowner may still be hated, but the man who has gone to the town and made a fortune, however modest, is admired and respected. The symbols of success are an air-conditioned house, a Peugeot, or even in some places just a bicycle or pair of trainers – but they demonstrate that the mould of poverty has been cracked, a great achievement. The status symbol is now almost universally *material* success.

Survivors of about my age have perforce more or less adjusted to these new times. But I believe we are mostly to some extent still disorientated; I wonder what greater traumas would be suffered by someone who had gone to sleep when I was born, and reawoke today.

During my eighty-plus years of life tumultuous upheavals have occurred on the large as well as the smaller or domestic scene.

The ghastly and pointless carnage of the first world war came at last, despite the folly of the generals, to an end. It was to change radically the map and the mind of Europe.

In 1917, the year after my birth, the USSR, the new Russian empire, the expression of a new political religion, came into existence. And it ended, its faith evaporated, in my old age.

When I was of an age to take part in it, the second world war broke out. Another terrible upheaval. These were indeed world wars. Not only were they fought throughout much of the globe, but the tremors are still shaking us.

After the second war came the age of decolonisation. In my youth a third of the world's land mass was coloured red in my school atlas, signifying the British Empire; by the late 1960s there were only a dozen or so tiny red dots on the map.

The USSR, until it disintegrated, and the USA bestrode the world as great and perilous world powers. They attacked each other with words and rattling weapons, but fought their actual battles by proxy in places like Angola and Ethiopia.

But after the end of the Cold War, when the USSR was basically just

Russia and the East European nations were freed from subjugation by their own efforts, new conflicts began to proliferate. It seemed as though the lifting of the threat of annihilation encouraged the minor actors to express their fears, hopes and hatreds by violence. This often took the form of senseless genocidal wars serving no serious purpose save the aggrandisement of some greedy and autistic warlord. In general, wars seem to have become more conflicts of peoples rather than regimes (including well-organised guerrilla movements) in which the combatants kill more for ethnic than for economic or territorial government policy reasons. In the Bosnian war for example, the old were brutalised for no possible military reason. The ethnicity of the conflict was illustrated by the Serbs destroying hundreds of mosques on the principle that they symbolised the cultural identity of the Muslim population, thus strengthening its morale. In Rwandan hospitals nurses marked the Tutsi babies to be killed when the holocaust started.

The following lines convey but little of a horrific genocidal massacre:

Ill at ease in mind and body
from the long jolting journey
and queasy anticipation,
we drag unwilling up the slope.
The stench engulfs us.
Rain just then begins,
weeping into mud
as we near the grave.
Slowly filing past,
slithering in the sludge,
cringing eyes peer aghast
into the reeking pit.

But to speak truthfully, some wars have been waged for an honourable cause, the liberation from a tyrant or foreign power; but how to measure the worth of political justice against the death and misery of obtaining it?

Altogether about one hundred million people, perhaps more, have died as a result of war since 1914. In the early years of the century ten per cent of the deaths were of noncombatants; in World War II, the percentage had gone up to forty; in Bosnia and other recent fields of carnage, it has risen to at least ninety. If you want your children to be safe, tell them to join the army!

But the violence was not only expressed in the form of warfare. In general the world has become more dangerous. Houses need much better locks if they are to claim insurance for the frequent burglaries. Crimes of violence are everywhere increasing.

Cities need much more serious policing. Groups which had lived together in peace suddenly turn upon each other. Torture is routinely inflicted, not just in interrogation, but to intimidate and indeed for the entertainment of the police or other captors. Capital punishment is restored where it had quite recently been prohibited.

The violence is also economic. The demands for cheap manufactured goods and for natural products like tea, coffee, rubber or out-of-season fruits drove the poor-nation clients of the rich to shameless exploitation of their workers. And of course this economic tyranny led from time to time to outbreaks of desperation, to be followed by ruthless suppression.

Tens of millions have been driven by force or fear from their homes to languish miserably in abysmal camps – if they were not murdered on the way.

And while our young men are shooting and hacking away at each other in the jungles of Africa, the paddy fields of South East Asia, the hills of Bosnia, or the icy uplands of Afghanistan, the timber companies are hacking away at the rainforests, industries of every sort are polluting the air and the waters, the chemicals of agribusiness are poisoning the soil, and most of us are using cars which ruin both the atmosphere of our cities and the ozone layer. But the relatively affluent really don't seem to worry very much so long as their lives are comfortable and the profits come rolling in.

Alienation

The speed and universality of change has created a widespread sense of alienation. The convulsions of our age have made us psychological nomads, not really belonging anywhere; aliens, in fact. The old social rules, even those which were repressive and unkind, told us where and who we were, gave us an identity however lowly – or at least something to defy and oppose. But everything has moved too fast for the new patterns of morality to emerge; this has given us freedoms but also deep anxieties often with related restraints! – and added to this was the menace of great wars, technical transformations which left us behind, and the loss of a faith which might have supported us. All this was vastly intensified for those living in areas of turbulence, huge social change such as decolonisation or the break-up of the state. These were heightened for many millions by the ghastly experiences of war, exile from their homes, insuperable poverty, incarceration in forced labour or concentration camps, endless fighting, endless loss and pain. Here the general alienation has tended to escalate into post-traumatic stress syndromes, so universal in a land like Bosnia as to appear normal.

At the same time and in some of the same societies – and perhaps others in which cultural differences make it hard for us to assess – the concentration on materialism, on profit, suggests the comparable emotional need. There is much distress to compensate for and the misapplied drive for happiness is very powerful and very widespread.

On the whole, I believe we have been profoundly altered. Looking back to different stages of my own life, I see a number of different Adam Curles. The character of the university student of that name is entirely alien to the octogenarian of today. We are immersed in problems we then did not know existed – and some of them didn't. We tend to be either nonbelievers or New Agers who will believe anything. We are intensely interested in gadgets, even more so in ourselves. We travel restlessly, but without wanting to understand the places we visit. We move equally restlessly from one sexual partner to another, but at the same time we easily become addicted to drugs or food or gambling. We are hard to please about most things. We deify the ego and its smallest whims. In a word, we are pretty unhappy.

The great hope had seemed to be the United Nations with its impressive array of special agencies. But though infinitely better then nothing, it has relatively failed. The United Nations, as we have seen, are sadly *dis*united. Although most of them, with a few exceptions, particularly the newer or smaller, have the same broad purposes, the achievement of these involves all too often rivalries and clashes. The disagreements and disastrously delayed agreements on Bosnia constitute a sad example. The recurrent Gulf clashes show that when things come to the crunch, the remaining superpower does what it wants – indeed, the protracted failure of the US to pay its UN dues is a sign of contempt which reduces confidence in it as a force for justice and stability in the world. Conversely, I take it as a badge of honour for UNESCO that both the UK and the US withdrew from its more independent and radical policies, although stigmatising these as wasteful, incompetent and biased.

How then can we diminish the force of the Hydra? We can argue for changes in taxation, we can campaign against the arms trade, but these and most of our other efforts are confined to attacking individual heads. We can make proposals for the reconstitution of the UN, for a global peacemaking agency, for a worldwide assault on poverty. But who will listen to us, or implement our proposals, however wise and rational, unless they conform to the standards of the culture of violence and profit?

But all this leaves the body, the great interdependency, virtually unharmed, indeed stronger because we have proved ineffective. But the centre of the Hydra's body, its heart, *is* the people. It is they upon whom all its activities and institutions depend. It is only they who can rescue our dwindling happiness from the morass of ignorance and fruitless attachments.

But the people, *they*, are really *WE*, for it is you and I who operate the systems through which the interdependency, the great *interessence*, the Hydra, exercises its power.

The rich and the poor

The profits have certainly been rolling in – at least until recently – for a considerable proportion of the people in the richer nations. At the same time, however, the less affluent proportion throughout the world has become relatively more and more indigent.

The exponentially growing scientific knowledge available to the rich, combined with huge technological skills, especially in processing and communications, has facilitated their exploitation of the world's natural resources – some irreplaceable – with great speed and efficiency. (This naturally raises the spectre of endless conflict over increasingly rare resources – especially water.)

The G7P nations, having all these resources, are not only wealthy but powerful and increasingly able to impose their will upon the poor countries of the world. Woe betide, for example, a poor Pacific nation (which, for its own benefit, I will not name) that objected to a US trawler fishing in its territorial waters. Eventually, after many requests, followed by warnings, a shell was fired across the bows of the intruder. Deeply affronted, the US launched a bitter economic and diplomatic war to teach the impertinent island a brutal lesson!

And within the poor nations themselves, those who serve the interests of the G7P use comparable techniques of control upon their own poor.

The great international financial agencies, such as the World Bank and the International Monetary Fund, being mainly financed and therefore influenced by their more affluent members, act as they advise. They promote money-making but often community-damaging (and therefore eventually money-losing) policies such as structural adjustment, and concentration on cash-crop agriculture which destroys traditional agriculture and with it social cohesion and healthily varied diet; this is now replaced, for those who can afford it, by costly and frequently less nutritious imported foodstuffs. (But of course in those countries trapped in the aimless bestiality of war, there is often famine – and no diet, healthy or not.)

The fortunate rich reject the idea that their affluence is founded on the indigence of others. On the contrary, they assert, they create wealth that then trickles down to enrich the poor. It is true that this could happen. But the rich control the political and economic system by which it might do so. Almost everywhere they block the channels down which the prosperity could flow to those who most need it. Consequently the poor in the 'less developed' countries have remained poor. Concurrently also, many of the G7P nations have tended to withdraw or to reduce support and privileges for the poorer classes (and nations; almost everywhere, even in altruistic Scandinavia, foreign aid has been reduced – the rich see no profit for them in it). And in the wealthier countries, for example the United Kingdom, redistribution of income through taxation has been brought to an end.

One difference between now and earlier centuries is that for the most part the social system was stable, not necessarily peaceful, but following certain patterns. It provided status, high or low, and identity. Now the system is cracked or fluid (choose your metaphor). Great things are held to be, and for many of us are, quite possible. But the implacable and impersonal free market promises so much, as the television shows us – and some of us are unable to share in it, to the detriment of a favourable and stable image of our own identity. By contrast, the earlier inequalities were perhaps sometimes, for some, more acceptable. We knew where we were, even though that place was harsh, and were less torn by the frustration of ever-vain aspiration. But who can tell?

To sum up, the current social economy contributes generally to the further exclusion and impotence of the poor. This results in blasted hope, in apathetic despair at perpetual poverty, depression, and in genuine physical hardship. Those most affected are frequently some group identifiable by language, colour or culture. Driven by desperation, they may try to change their lot by violence. But war leads to further ills – to famine, disease and homelessness, and to the morass of alienation. The knowledge that there is enormous wealth and power for some is a constant exacerbation for those lacking them: here are the roots of the bush wars of Africa, the Moscow Mafia, the underworld of Rio.

It is obvious that the poor play little overt part, except for their usually exploited labour, in the great economic, military and political interdependency we are calling the Hydra. Nevertheless they form a part of its total impact on the world. They have been touched by the breath of affluence. They are aware of – though they may not have experienced – the delights of refrigeration, of cars, of television. They have accepted the Hydra's values, even if they cannot join its culture of wealth and profit. Like their rulers who resent inability to join the nuclear club, they are angry at their exclusion from what they might well consider to be their rights. Those who achieve an education know well that the wealthy speak glibly of human rights, unaware that their policies all too often deprive the poor of the most basic rights to food, health and shelter.

Thus the poor, while suffering the depredations of the Hydra, are in a sense a part of it, both enlarging and complicating its culture of violence.

These last few pages have told a sorry story. However, it is not only, or not so much, what people do to each other – for most people behave decently – but what they *think* about the matter. They accept that there is more violence, more war, much inequality; and they put up with it – what else can they do? They think that in the last resort violence is justified – it works, doesn't it? After all, we have to look after our interests in the Gulf, don't we? This is the culture of violence, the Hydra in action.

Evening is sour, the cold light slides oblique
between and around what should
be decently buried respectfully mourned,
lighting up grotesque bodies tortured
out of agonised existence
limbs or genitals mashed or missing
braised among smouldering tyres,
or dangling jerking necks kinked
from trees that should bear fruit,
or simply heads stuck on spikes around
the university, that centre of culture
where you can easily obtain
a masters degree of inhumanity.
Have mercy have mercy upon them
especially the tormentors
for they know full well
what they are doing
and enjoy it greatly
laughing merrily the while.
Have mercy on the civil servant
proud of his accuracy,
marking up the tally of the slain.
Have mercy on the officer
who nods approval, commenting
Jolly good show.
Finally darkness falls.
The light at the end of the tunnel
flickers and dies out;
there is no healing night,
only cover for more killing.

4

Changing the Hydra

Taming the Hydra

To tame and transform the Hydra means to tame and transform ourselves, or at least our illusions of acquisition and anger. The first steps towards doing that are to learn about the creature and our relationship to it. That is the chief subject of this book. As we understand more and more about our thrall of the monster, it may be easier to visualise what life would be like without the wars, injustices, oppressions, divisive inequalities, and pollutions – physical and moral – with which it has plagued us.

But we have to realise that a tamed Hydra is not a dead Hydra; we are not Hercules intent on slaughter; that would be self-destruction! The Hydra represents interdependency, the essence of everything in life. Our task is to ensure that its elements are oriented to the advantage of all rather than a few; that their purpose and aspirations are changed rather than their skills and abilities, which are constructive and creative.

Most of the Scandinavian countries, for example, have made substantial moves in the direction of this change, but are held back by being part of a global system that has not, and which consequently drags them down towards its own level. Britain has currently constructive aspirations to be free of these ills, but may be greatly held back by its class structure and a lingering faith in militarism. But by contrast with most of Europe, the majority of countries of Africa, Latin America and Asia have hardly made a start; shamefully, it is the rich ones of Europe and North America that are largely responsible for retarding these – and by the same token, themselves.

A tamed Hydra would not only remove many of such ills as war and gross inequalities from the world, but satisfy our deepest more personal needs. True development of a human group, whether community or nation, need – and indeed *should* – not be measured in terms of wealth or even (which is better) social criteria such as education and life expectancy. More revealing are conditions which together contribute most to our general well-being. Here is a way of classifying these in terms of five words beginning with the letter S.

The first is *Sufficiency.* This means that we have enough employment, nutritious food, adequate shelter, health care, education, family stability, etc. to provide a strong physical and mental basis for the full development of our potential.

Then *Satisfaction*, meaning that all these sufficiencies are provided in a pleasant fashion – for example, that the nutritious food is also tasty, that education is interesting and imaginatively stimulating, and that there is ample scope for enjoyable communal activities.

Thirdly, *Safety* or *Security*, that is to say secure in the knowledge that there will be no war, no marauding warlords, no corrupt or unaccountable police, no death squads; more positively, that one can rely on the judicial system, that provision will be ensured for those suffering medical or financial crises beyond the range of family assistance.

Next, *Stimulus* in the sense of encouragement and opportunity to follow personal talents and interests in work, art and other creative fields of study or sport.

Lastly, *Service*. This particularly means the chance to take some role in the ordering of local, national, or international affairs. In the so-called Western democracies we do, of course, have such opportunities. However, the possibility of playing an active part is limited for many to casting an occasional vote, and the image of the councillor or member of parliament is in many places so tarnished that few of us are drawn to public office, except for the flawed motive of personal advantage.

It is clear that adequate satisfaction of these needs will involve a most profound restructuring of at least a part of all existing societies; a long, difficult and dangerous affair. Add work to remove the threat of war and weapons of mass destruction, and humanity has a stupendous task. But the alternative is infinitely worse.

We should remember, however, that many countries have attempted recently to remake themselves, for instance, a majority of post-independence African nations, especially those which unwisely chose Western-type democratic constitutions. These failed for two reasons. The new constitutions were alien to local traditions of governance; and the new leaders carried on the practices of their predecessors – black men sat on seats of power still warm from white bums. But at least they demonstrated the ability to make a vast effort. It didn't work, but it showed what might. Those of us in the West have also had the benefit of object lessons: the eventual shambles of both far right and far left.

One lesson for all is that although every large group, with its own dominant lifestyle forged over generations, must not deviate too much from the existing pattern, it can still learn something from the experience of others. Although I would not dare to suggest major constitutional reform for Britain, I think we have something positive to learn from, say, South Africa, Norway and Scottish plans for devolution; just as we should heed negative lessons from Chile, Colombia, Serbia, Sri Lanka and the USSR.

It is even harder for me to say anything about the development of a national and particularly an international economic structure that provides for the supply of agricultural and industrial products to ensure *Sufficiency*. And does so, moreover, without a market approach that will further impoverish those regions that are already indigent, but at the same time will not enrich its shareholders as flagrantly as hitherto.

This, and many other changes in practice that will be essential to the effectiveness of every innovation, cannot occur without a comparable change in personal values. The first seeds of this revolution in feeling have certainly begun to germinate in everyone whose thoughts are green or in anyway 'left wing'. I would not like to think, however, that such changes have to be considered as 'political' or 'environmental', but as true expressions of our humanity. Politics, the economy and issues of the environment are obviously essential, but are to be considered in the wider context of the interdependency. This is the spirit in which I have written these pages.

But these things will only begin to grow as we begin to understand the Hydra and try to take some action to transform it.

Taming ourselves

Paradoxically, those aspects of the Hydra jigsaw puzzle that are most intractable and most central to completing it, are those nearest to us – ourselves. We are both a part of and apart from it. We may have a small role in resolving the great issues, but we – rather than some specific issue that may appear dominant – are most directly responsible where we are concerned. For example, I have occasionally been involved as a go-between in a violent conflict in which a key decision maker is faced with a momentous choice, such as whether to continue to fight, or to make peace. He has to weigh up many difficult aspects of the military, political, and economic situation. The atmosphere may be tense and angry; he may be exhausted. What can I do to help him make a decision which is wise and humane?

As a foreigner I cannot say anything helpful about his domestic political worries; I can't give economic or military advice. All I can do is to offer him friendship and the temporary haven of a relationship which is understanding, supportive and undemanding. This may to some small extent lower his inner tension and reduce his anxiety so that he can reflect more peacefully and profoundly on the situation. He may then make a much better decision than he would have done if he had been harried by frightened ministers, or suffering personal stress, or feeling resentful and desperate. His decision in that case might have been less the fruit of wisdom than of anger, desire for revenge, hopelessness, or pressures from his advisers.

In all of this, my state of mind may have been helpful. But then I and of course all of us, as paid up (in)voluntary members of this Hydra-dominated society, are constantly faced with difficult problems. What, for example, do we do about the beguilingly lavish lifestyle we are constantly being offered? How do we guide our children through the moral labyrinth – or ourselves for that matter? How should we avoid being sucked into the capitalist maelstrom – but we are already in it, aren't we? How do we get out? Or don't we want to?

In fact my state of mind is likely to be as distracted, as confused and curdled with such negative emotions as self-pity, self-satisfaction, angst, prejudice and ambiguity, as those of anyone we might want to help. Shafts of these disturbed feelings flicker across the screen of consciousness so constantly as to be almost unnoticed. Only when exacerbating circumstances arise does anxiety change to fear, prejudice to hatred, self-pity to depression, and so on. All the time, however, we are the victims of feelings which cloud awareness and block off the great sources of wisdom and compassion. How does this happen? It is presumably the function of continuous electrical activity in the brain linking or triggering circuits of memories, many of which are associated with childhood pain or anxiety. It is thus that our potential value to our friends, and theirs to us, is greatly reduced – this is the situation which might be termed feeding off each other's neuroses.

One reason for this condition could be thought of as our mechanical function. From birth we learn to do things without thought. From the moment when, as a baby, we first try to use a spoon, to the day when we learn to carry out the most delicate and dexterous operations like playing the piano, driving a car, or using a computer, we are trying to do it without thought – and to a considerable extent succeeding. Imagine how impossible life would be if, whenever we dressed ourselves, we had to work out, all over again, how to do up buttons or tie shoe laces! But we sacrifice a slice of our freedom for this boon: we become semi-conscious slaves to our mental mechanism which takes over like the automatic pilot of a plane – which cannot be programmed to cope with all emergencies! Moreover, because a large proportion of our mental equipment is connected with the imprint and hence the fantasies of pain, there is an element of sickness and distortion also affecting our conscious thought.

The powerful antidote to these ills is awareness (see also pages 88–89). Awareness means being *fully conscious, awake, watchful.* I understood the teachings of the Gospels better when I read the instructions of Jesus to the disciples: *I say to you and I say to all: Watch.* It is essential to watch if we are not to be invaded by illusions and negativities that poison our potential. The Buddhist equivalent is similar: some students approached a wise teacher seeking guidance. He simply said: *Attention.* When asked to enlarge on this, he just repeated, *Attention, Attention, Attention.*

To do this is infinitely harder than to realise its necessity. It means, essentially, understanding the content of our mind at the most profound level, something of course that is the basis of the depth psychologies of Freud, Jung and their many diverse followers; it is the essence of all meditation. It awakens our capacities and controls the vultures of ego, fear and hatred, let alone the other minor predators of irritation and pique. The more aware are we at any given moment (the level fluctuates) the more we can help other people to see through disabling illusions. We do not need to say very much, but this is a better service than 'practical' advice.

There are many methods of heightening awareness, but the simplest is to seek some device for *remembering* to remember oneself, to observe with detachment what is happening in one's mind, to try to empty it.

My shelter for the night,
this sleazy Madras hotel.
Bare bulb reluctantly illuminates
the shame-faced room,
the fan can hardly shift
air heavy with damp
and cockroach farts
(they rush around aghast, their midnight
scavenging aborted).

He stands barefooted in the door,
white uniform starched clean
but somewhat threadbare,
to see if I'm materially all right –
mosquito net set up,
bed turned down, water flowing, if rusty,
from the tap:

nothing is said.

He turns on me his lambent gaze;
a shaft of compassion and acceptance
slams me with the million volts
of Buddhahood.

Empty of presumption
of what we call self,
full of the universe,
we contain each other.

5

Happiness

The title of this chapter speaks for itself, but the concept of happiness as applied to issues of conflict, peace and social change is perhaps new. For me, however, it symbolises the central issues we shall be discussing and so is introduced at some length here.

For a number of years I have been preoccupied with the relationship between what we *are* and what we *do*, our inner and our outer lives. The concept of happiness has been for me the key for unlocking the sad mysteries of inner hatred and outer violence. The reason for this is that true happiness implies freedom from many of those illusions that cloud the essence of our nature, of which happiness is surely a part. Enlightened by it, we can see that anger, fear, hatred and ambition which lead to violence reside in our own minds; any quarrel is a clash of misconceptions. For this reason, happiness is an essential element in the struggle to erode violence; although the work may be hard and the conditions in which it is carried out grimly sombre, it is impassioned by a longing for the happiness of others.

If these ideas may sound strange, I should explain that as a half psychologist (the other half is anthropologist) I believe that the pursuit of happiness, as Jefferson put it, is a dominant and universal human drive.

But why happiness rather than some other strong human drive, such as sex, or survival, or protective aggression against predators or sexual rivals? My reason is that the quest is the basis of everything we do. Even if what we do is unpleasant, boring, dangerous or painful, *not doing it would be even worse.* Shame or guilt at our laziness or cowardice would, we feel, bring even more unhappiness than doing the displeasing job. What is at stake, then, is preserving as much happiness as is possible in the circumstances.

Our feelings about what we should do or not do – that is, basically, about what will make us more, or less, happy – are greatly affected by our culture. Paradoxically, in a virtually atheist society our moral code is one that was largely implanted in the social culture by the churches; some of their underlying principles, such as original sin, play a part in the confusion of life today.

Unfortunately, just because happiness is so powerful, it may easily swerve off course to bring about its antithesis. If things go wrong, we blame the circumstances or other people, not realising that the degree of happiness is also a reflection of our own inner state – and so may often be more important than the actual situation. But not understanding this, our efforts to make up for disappointment or frustration can lead inexorably to a fresh cycle of pain, anger or despair.

But what, we may ask, has this to do with happiness? In one sense, of course, nothing. In another, everything; it is the quest for happiness turned upside down.

Happiness, I say again, is a drive. Or, to put it another way, it expresses an urge to restore the primal happiness with which, as William Blake knew, we are born: 'I have no name/I am but two days old'./What shall I call thee?/ 'I happy am,/Joy is my name'. And such happiness is shared by other species, as all know who have watched lambs or puppies playing. But it tends not to last because we do not properly understand it and so misuse it. Sex is a similarly powerful drive; it can bring wonderful joy and harmony, or the most bitter unhappiness and distortion.

But what are we really discussing? Happiness is far less easy to define than those conditions which have an apparently largely physical basis, like hunger or perhaps even fear. But however we try to describe it, whatever we think of as happiness is hugely significant, judging by the frequent references to it. Here is a selection of these.

JEREMY BENTHAM: The greatest Happiness for the greatest number is the foundation of morals and legislation.

ARISTOTLE: Happiness is an expression of the soul in considered action.

DOSTOEVSKY: Happiness does not lie in happiness, but in the achievement of it.

JOHN KEATS: Wherein lies happiness? In that which becks/ Our ready minds to fellowship divine/ A fellowship with essence till we shine/ Full alchemised and full of space. Behold/ The clear religion in the heaven.

THE XIVTH DALAI LAMA: I believe that the very purpose of our life is to seek happiness ... the very motion of our life is towards happiness.

BERTHOLD BRECHT: The right to happiness is fundamental. Men live so little time and die alone.

GEORGE SANTAYANA: Happiness is the only sanction of life.

IMMANUEL KANT: Virtue and happiness constitute the *summum bonum* of life.

EMILE ZOLA: I have one passion only for light in the name of humanity which has borne so much and has a right to happiness.

ALEXANDER POPE: Oh happiness, our being's aim and end.

THOMAS JEFFERSON: I consider these truths to be self-evident, that all men are equal, that they are endowed by their Creator with certain unalienable Rights, and that among these are Life, Liberty and the pursuit of Happiness.

These quotations, and many others, support my belief that the pursuit of happiness, to use Jefferson's term, is truly a drive, a main-spring of human energy as powerful as sex (which is in part one of its manifestations, the two being indeed very closely associated). The pursuit of happiness, like the quest for sexual gratification, can lead us to bliss or to realms of illusion and fantasy. When powerful energies are involved, both miracles and disasters often occur. But wherever the drive for happiness, and/or our illusions about the nature of happiness, may lead us, it must be reckoned an enormous force.

And one which is universal. It can be recognised in its least adulterated form in the play of young animals. Also in human babies – the fact that they also often cry may be attributed, at least in part, to the frustrations of their helplessness as compared with the mobility of most young creatures. In terms of psychoanalysis the pleasure principle (the Freudian term for the drive for happiness) is deeply rooted in the unconscious, the Id, impelling us to action, however disastrous.

Legitimacy of the happiness concept

Happiness may, of course, be eclipsed or at least weakened by many things: by childhood neglect or abuse, by violence or indigence, or by perverse example, by sickness – or simply and perhaps almost universally, by ignorance.

However, instead of now considering what drives it off course, let us consider its source. Here I must depart from the analytic assumption of a blind and essentially selfish happiness drive and posit a more positive human nature, one having a great potential for wisdom, generosity and compassion. This potential can perhaps best be cultivated by social or personal example, by wise education, and by the awakened consciousness of the individual.

Why should you agree with this approach? I can offer no 'proof', except to say that I have found it to be true. I have met a number of men and women whose acts, and our traditions, would encourage us to think of them as 'bad', but invariably, if they were dealt with generously and justly, their latent humanity and 'goodness' was evoked.

Also, of course, many of the world's great philosophies and religions have stressed our wonderful latent capacities. Buddhism, which is both agnostic and noncredal (the Buddha stressed that we must work things out for ourselves) and less a religion than a psycho/philosophical system, is pre-eminent in this respect. It holds that all beings have the Buddha nature. Neither is any action called 'sinful'. Instead, it is branded 'unskilful', that is to say an unskilful means of attaining the goal of understanding, of being aware of the nature of reality (this is often referred to as enlightenment, but this gives it a falsely mystical nuance). Our endowment is claimed to be inherently perfect in the sense that our *machinery*, our *physical and mental equipment*, is essentially perfect. But we forget, misuse and become deluded about it.

Christianity is superficially very different. There is considerable stress on 'sin' as being 'original', though Paul and Augustine, rather than Jesus, must take most of the blame for the concept. The idea of innate wickedness has caused many millions to feel badly about themselves, and abjectly to pray forgiveness for the apparently unavoidable fact that 'there is no health in us'. But many Christians also think of the 'Christ nature' and the 'Christ within', which is not so different from the Buddhist belief.

So far as I am aware, no major religious system, certainly not Islam, Hinduism or Judaism, has any belief similar to original sin. Equally, however, not all would teach the basic goodness of human nature, except perhaps some versions of Hinduism and Sufic Islam. (I should mention, however, that religion is not the only source of guilt feelings. They are often based on ill-treatment or neglect in infancy which makes a young child feel unlovable and therefore wicked, because it would otherwise be loved by its parents.)

In the realm of depth psychology, psychoanalysis particularly emphasises the inexorable inner conflict of good and evil (though the eminent John Bowlby asserts that 'humans are pre-programmed to develop in a socially co-operative way'). Less so, however, those such as Jung in his analytical psychology, and Assagioli in his psychosynthesis, who go perhaps even further than the Buddhists in what some call (I personally question the term) *spiritual* psychology. So do various other forms of depth psychology including the transpersonal and humanistic, also Eastern psychophilosophies such as various forms of yoga.

Once we accept that we are born with a basically pristine nature, we can without prejudice consider the psychology of *happiness*.

Primal happiness

Firstly, we are born happy (apart from the potentially damaging character of birth). We experience *primal* happiness. This is a condition we rarely experience in adult life. It is pure joy, inseparable from any outside circumstances. It may come quite unexpectedly, on awaking perhaps from sleep. It can only be described as unalloyed delight in being alive.

But our initially pristine nature does not normally remain so for long. We are born into a web of relationship with parents, siblings and other close family members; this is our earliest educational experience. We learn from it what is good and what is bad, and since the behavioural idiom of all families differs, we all learn slightly different things and in a slightly – or indeed sometimes, greatly – different manner.

In particular we learn how to strive towards happiness in adverse circumstances which, moreover, we do not understand. We make mistakes. What we thought would bring an euphoric response has the opposite effect. What we hoped would arouse pity merely irritates.

In the face of adult or sibling disfavour, we build up defences which may only make things worse – and us more unhappy – so that a miserable cycle of mutual aggravation becomes habitual, and primal happiness obscured.

Of course the story is not all so grim. Care, sensitivity – and it must be admitted good luck, may create a very happy milieu in which the child may develop without conflict or manipulation.

In this case s/he will grow up with the original endowment of wisdom, generosity and compassion much less damaged than that of those who have had to struggle and in a sense distort their nature to obtain – or indeed to fail to obtain – a quota of happiness. But we have to admit that this is very much a matter of degree. Some have had to strive for happiness (and generally speaking, the more we struggle the more we fail) harder than others; but none escape without any effort. Everyone's capacity for enjoyment of pure primal happiness is impaired.

Existential happiness

A type of happiness which is somewhat less intense and less unusual I would refer to as *existential* happiness. This is felt, in my limited experience, after some difficult or dangerous ordeal. It does not, however, relate to the ordeal, which fades into the mental background. I assume that some combination of relief and relaxed tension breaks through the veil of misconception and externalisation that obscures the primal source. It is important to recognise that both primal and existential happiness differ from what we shall discuss in the following paragraphs in that they do not make demands, they are self-sufficient.

Conditional happiness

This is not the case with two related forms of the drive. Both are *conditional* in the sense of the *if* qualification; if I had ... could ... knew ... etc., I would be happy. These are divided into the *rational* and the *ignorant.*

The rational conditional (apologies for the cumbersome terms) drive for happiness is felt by those who need what is necessary to fulfil themselves and care for the essential needs of their families for such things as food, shelter, health care, education and justice. When these are satisfied, a far greater quota of primal happiness is restored.

By contrast the drive I term 'ignorant' is towards goals that, in the material though not the psychological sense, are non-essential. They are for recognition, popularity, admiration, envy and similar ego-boosters. The means of achieving these would, for example, be through owning a new car, going on holiday to fashionable resorts, keeping a good cellar, the tasteful decor of one's home and, in general, possessions, position and power.

The drive adapts to different levels and types of culture and sophistication. I knew one unfortunate man who had spent many years in gaol for trivial offences. His proud boast was that it had been a maximum security prison, not any ordinary clink, where his friends had been the Great Train Robbers.

The main purpose of this distorted aspect of the drive for happiness is to enable us to look in the mental mirror and to like what we see; to free us of the feelings of worthlessness and guilt arising, perhaps, from experiences that have made us feel unloved, and so in great need of the reassurance of popularity and approval.

An additional and perhaps more universal source is the sense of having lost or failed to cultivate our wonderful inner potential. This is often felt as a poignant but unidentified bereavement.

I must emphasise that the differentiation between the two conditional drives is not in any sense judgemental. Virtually everyone experiences both according to the shifting circumstances of their lives. If the conditions that emphasise the rational should improve, we may enjoy the 'luxury' of the irrational drive with its ego-serving aspirations and desires. The more we do so, however, the more is our peace of mind jeopardised and the true primal source of happiness obscured.

The gratification obtained from both conditional drives, particularly the ignorant drive, is likely, because of ever-changing conditions both material and emotional, to be short-lived. We are commonly deluded into *feeling,* although we intellectually *know* this to be untrue, that conditions in which we are happy will last for ever.

Our gratification is based on a second illusion: that happiness depends on external circumstances. I was disillusioned about this at the age of five. I longed for a particular toy – a gun, in fact! This my mother at first refused to give me, yielding at last, however, to my importuning. Now, I said to myself, I shall be happy forever, I shall never want anything again. But a few days later I found myself in tears over some trivial mishap. I realised I had been wrong; I saw that happiness did not come from outside but from within.

Wanting and yearning

The main difference between primal and existential happiness on the one hand, and on the other the conditional happiness drives, is that the latter are inseparable from *wanting* and *yearning*; where these are present, there is potential conflict and violence. Issues of identity are often involved with desiring and thus easily side-step into rivalry and hostility.

This almost invariably generates a potentially vicious cycle in which the chances of true happiness are enormously diminished through the very drives which emanate from primal happiness.

Visualise a circle. One point on it is labelled Ignorance and Illusion, another is marked Longing, Desiring, Lust or other comparable words, a third is designated Hatred, Anger, Dislike etc. Start anywhere, but Ignorance is perhaps easiest. It means ignorance of our true nature, our basic identity, which is our great potential for happiness, wisdom, and compassion. This, however, is to some extent clouded over, as we shall see as we progress round the circle.

Next comes Longing. This is the attempt to compensate for the loss of happiness, and forgetfulness of the true nature, by getting things or arranging situations which will serve as substitutes. But these all fail later, or probably sooner.

The failure of Longing to assuage our pain disturbs and distresses us. We feel Anger or Resentment towards the people or situations on which we pin responsibility for our failures.

These negative emotions further obscure the source of happiness and our other great potential qualities; the yearning desire for something to make up for our loss grows stronger, but our increasingly frantic efforts fail yet more bitterly; our furious Hatred grows; our illusions become more obsessive... round and round it goes.

Threats to happiness: externality and identity

As we mature we tend to become infected with what might be termed externality (the second great illusion referred to above)): the happiness drive turns hopefully towards the enjoyment and manipulation of what is outside us. These things are not only *not* the *source* of happiness, however good they may be, but what they *are* is inherently impermanent. Thus they become the occasion for disappointment, frustration, desperation, the sense of loss and, perhaps in the end, rage and violence.

This illusion, however, not only affects our happiness, but the character of our whole civilisation. Over long periods of time, these externalities may become crystallised in military or economic or social institutions, or in traditions which to a considerable extent freeze our expectations, and consequently patterns of behaviour, in a relatively lasting fashion. We expect to have more and more wars, so we create and maintain armies, staff colleges, intelligence agencies. We expect to carry out our affairs with money, so we create and maintain banks, stock exchanges, corporations (but what if, instead, we used barter and exchange of services? What if the taking of interest, as still in some Islamic banks and in early Christianity, were illegal?). The symbiosis of our need for happiness and the external means we devise for its satisfaction, contribute to destruction and rivalry throughout the world.

But the essence of joy, the great happiness potential, is an integral part of our nature. Though obscured by preoccupation with externalities as memory may be by alcohol, its primal source still pervades our being with its warmth. It may, however, feel like central heating set very low; and the greater the obscuration, the deeper the chill.

Paradoxically, however, although the peaceful joy of primal happiness is dimmed, the great driving force, the 'pursuit of happiness', persists. In fact, its degree of power is the very function of its failure. The urge to achieve, to have, to be, to overcome what is wrong with our lives, becomes stronger with our lack of success. We want these things, however paltry. Without them we feel we are to a greater or lesser extent empty, incomplete, uneasy – in a word *unhappy*. No matter that what we want is trivial, to the degree that we desire it, we feel it is the one condition of happiness. But being based on externals it is fragile and evanescent and, at best, simply a state of less pain. But it may, of course, lead to something of terrible import – the crazed ambition of a Hitler!

A major aspect of the ignorant drive, which like the others, affects almost all of us to some degree, is the quest for identity. We long to feel we are *someone*, to be identified as distinguished by a particular set of qualities. We all have an idea of who we are. It is cobbled together of things which belong to us or to which we belong. What seems to us to be distinctive may be our appearance, our education, our particular skills or profession, our family and so on and so on. These locate us in society and, if we are important enough, in the world – but of course for some unfortunates a sad self-image locates them in a rather miserable spot.

Our identity is partly a conscious and partly an unconscious construct. We take an open pride in being the woman or man who has achieved this or that. When we prepare our c.v. for a job application we marshal all the facts we think will make a good impression – carefully tempered not to sound too boastful. This much is of course conscious. I recall, however, how my award of a certain academic honour unconsciously affected my self-view. I was working with a group of exceptionally brilliant people and from time to time suffered a displeasing sense of inferiority. When this happened, however, a ray of comfort from an unknown source would lighten my depression. It was months before I realised that my largely forgotten award (not shared by most of the others) suggested I was not as stupid as I feared I must be.

Most importantly, our identity gives us a sense of our own *reality.* This is ME, and I am separate from and different from you. But this is another illusion to obscure our perception of reality and to cover primal happiness with the fog of ignorance.

We are not simply the product of our parents' genes, but of our whole human environment, its culture, teachers, our experiences, the artistic and philosophical influences that have played on us. All of these are incorporated in our being, just as our being is incorporated into that of countless others. Every change in our circumstances also changes us. Today I am different from what I was yesterday – how much more so last year, a decade ago, a half century ago. How differently I feel and act with people I love from how I do on formal occasions; when being professional and when being social; when jolly and when miserable; thoughtful or frivolous.

Who, in fact, am I? What is my true identity – indeed, do I have one?

We shield ourselves from these awkward questions because we base much of our social philosophy and psychological belief upon the traditional concept of 'I'. The prospect of recognising it as a fiction is very alarming.

It is, however, necessary, if we are to understand how to deal with the problems of violence, hatred and despair which are largely the subject of these pages. It is necessary to do so if we are to enjoy fully our birthright of happiness.

First of all I should say that the deconstruction of the self as a completely self-existent, separate entity does not mean that you and I do not exist as recognisable individuals.

The nature of our being can be perhaps best *re*constructed by analogy with the Tibetan parable of Indra's net described in the following short poem.

At each intersection of the endless net
of Indra's heaven, according to the myth,
there is a bead that represents a life.
Each bead reflects every other
and every reflection of every other.
In the sub-atomic field every hadron
affects and is affected by all the rest,
resulting in a flux of energy and movement
in which little can be foretold
save unpredictability and endless change.

The boundaries between us are hallucinations,
we are indeed members of one another,
dancing together spontaneously like the hadrons,
containing each other like the beads.

We do in fact possess unique individuality, but it is an individuality forged from the flow of energy and wisdom from countless multidirectional sources, playing upon our original inherited endowment; a wonderful paradox of unity in diversity, an endless source of happiness.

Money and wealth

These words exemplify another of the great illusions. Advertisements for lotteries and other money-making schemes show the successful investors grinning, prancing, or expressing other physical symptoms of supposed great happiness. In fact, what many people believe they want most of all is money, equating money with joy. However, except when cash enables us to save a sick child or avoid some dreadful adversity, money of itself does not stave off misery. This is something known to us all, but we do not act on that knowledge.

We should, however, learn better. Unless some means is found on controlling the speculation that is devastating the world's markets, we may all face poverty and must learn to live with it without loss of happiness.

But loss of money does not mean loss of wealth. The wealth that enables us to live richly is the cultivation of our great inner resources of wisdom, loving appreciation, and the deep primal happiness. These are far more than compensatory substitutes for crass cash; they are the true stuff of life, the real stuff of all these pages.

Discussion

To end this chapter, I should explain further the relevance of happiness to an examination of the Hydra and the culture of violence.

The degree of clarity of primal happiness is like a thermometer measuring our ability to deal constructively with these things. This source of happiness does not, of course, depend on circumstances, it is not conditional. It is happiness unrelated to the satisfaction of cravings – which are often very evanescent and *always* impermanent, usually leading to unhappiness, more craving, more disappointment, more unhappiness…

The more free we are of the illusions of the ignorant conditional drive and of the false identity associated with it, the more we are liberated to transform the Hydra and to erode its related culture.

The extent, frequently mentioned, of our own implication with the Hydra depends on the extent to which we are entrapped by these illusions. This in turn depends to some extent on the shifting flow of circumstances, but – as with seasonal temperature – we tend to have an average degree of hallucination. The higher it is, the less our capacity for sustained positive action; and the lower, the greater.

It is often said that our age is particularly materialistic. In the clumsy terms used here, this would suggest domination by the ignorant conditional drive; a great need for and strong expectation of happiness gained from acquisition.

Although it is not hard to assess addiction to consumerism in individuals, it is very difficult to judge whole societies in this respect. Nevertheless, I have known communities in which people who *had* very little *seemed to want* very little, but appeared, contrary to what might be expected in the West, happy and high-spirited.

By contrast it appears, superficially at least, that the members of our high consumption society are less relaxed and light-hearted than, for example, my beloved Chakmas before their communal destruction. This suggests that we are more overwhelmed by, and by the same token, less able to resist the allure of the glamorous opportunities of the Hydra and the culture of violence.

I should emphasise my belief that it is possible for us to lower the average threshold of craving, of the ignorant conditional drive. Or, if the circumstances provoking self-pity, fear, vanity or longing are aggravated, to raise it. I have pondered the usefulness of suggesting measures for lowering the threshold. However, there is such a variety of measures suited to an equal variety of individuals that this could simply prove confusing. I will only say that the essence of virtually all approaches is *awareness*.

I hope I have shown clearly the significant interconnectedness of Hydra and happiness. Because of our failures of understanding, our happiness drive easily degenerates to the ignorant conditional – we shall be happy *IF* ... we have, or can do this, that or the other particular thing. If we can only achieve this at the expense of another, *tant pis.* Slaves, for example, have seemed particularly desirable acquisitions to increase our prosperity in some places at certain stages, beginning perhaps in Babylon and continuing in various ways until today, and until recently in South Africa.

(It could be argued that, rather than happiness, the love that 'makes the world go round' should be considered as the greatest clue to understanding violent, as well as tender and cooperative human behaviour. It certainly is one of the great clues; without doubt, moreover, love and happiness are inextricably interwoven at the summit of human bliss. It is, however, also a complex and contradictory clue, in large part because of the sex factor, also because it had been romanticised in so many and such diverse ways. Happiness, as I understand and have tried to explain it, can be more clearly analysed and directly related to experience.)

Postscript

It may seem surprising that the word *peace* has hardly appeared in these chapters. It is a complex and confusing concept, very often used simply to indicate the end of fighting. However, this would leave us with a very limited and shallow view of the condition. Some decades ago I coined the terms peaceful and unpeaceful relations as applying to any relationship from the transpersonal to the transnational in which, if peaceful, the parties did each other more good than harm; and if unpeaceful, the other way around.

It may be that in thinking of happiness, I am referring to one component of peace or peaceful relations. Certainly the two are very compatible, perhaps sometimes identical.

Nevertheless, my vision of happiness is of an all-embracing cheerfulness and confidence, a joyous acceptance of life; the French phrase *joie de vivre* is highly significant. This is a quality I find rare even among those whose relationships with everyone are delightfully warm and friendly. But apart from this, what I think of as happiness adds a zip, a zest. It has a force most urgently needed to impact the world, and it seems to me to be in very short supply.

Many possible reasons for this lack are embedded in the personal history of women and men, but it is heightened by their belief that there is nothing they can do, that they are helpless against the implacable forces of militarism or the market.

But these essentially peaceful people must be transformed into *powerful* people eager to struggle valiantly against the rule of the Hydra, not in order themselves to dominate or control, but to turn the focus of its undoubted energies to peacefully creative action. With this in mind, they must first recognise and then cultivate the tremendous strength and wisdom of their own nature.

The sky featureless and chill,
too sad for tears of rain.
The village shattered and empty,
beset by drab fields, untilled, unsown
save by mines lurking to destroy,
and the dead, those poor bodies,
waiting to be found
and given due respect
after the cruel killing
and the crude disposal.
Our hearts anaesthetised for this,
benumbed by what's beyond
imagination.
No talking – nothing to say.
We walk innerly alone,
wanting no companion.
I go behind a ruined house to pee,
some comfort in this living act
amid the desolation.

6

Mind, system and society

To transform the force of the Hydra, it is not only necessary for us to understand it, but also for us to understand certain aspects of our own minds, since we are not only the assailants but also in many ways the partners of the monster. It is equally important to understand the context in which we collectively operate: society, both local and global.

In the nineteenth century neuroscientists tended to consider that there was a close connection between the brain and mind, indeed that the brain was the organ of mind, but opinion is now much more open. Two men were largely responsible for laying the foundations for current wide ranging speculations on the nature of mind.

Dissipative systems – Prigogine

One was Ilya Prigogine, a chemist who won the Nobel Prize in 1974 for his work on what he referred to as 'dissipative structures'. He coined this term to refer to systems which maintain their own structure by breaking down others in the course of metabolism, as of course we do in eating. This creates the disorder of entropy which is eventually 'dissipated' as waste products. This description was first applied to chemical systems, but later studies widened the concept to cover living systems capable of self-regulation, even, in the case of social systems, of creative adaptation.

The concept of social systems aroused some controversy at one stage. Ecosystems regulate themselves through multiple feedback loops in which waste is used to fuel new cycles. But what is the equivalent in social systems? What serves in human systems to nourish fresh growth instead of animal droppings, dead foliage and so on? Language has been suggested as a substitute, but perhaps also it is old ideas, patterns of behaviour, beliefs, etc. that fall into decay, stimulating debate, dissent and emerging new alternatives.

Mind – Bateson

The second scholar who contributed greatly to our understanding of mind was Gregory Bateson. He was an English anthropologist/philosopher with an intense interest in the workings of mind, which he studied in many different settings, especially in the natural world and in very diverse cultures. He held that mind was a property of all living things, including ones without brains, such as molecules, that had faculties of memory and learning. He expressed this view pithily: 'mind is the essence of being alive'; mind could be seen as the ability of any organism to assess and respond appropriately to, say, changes in temperature or humidity. (Working independently, he reached the same conclusions as neuroscientist Humberto Maurana in Chile in the late 1960s.)

If mind is the capacity of all living organisms to react adaptively, humans will tend, sooner or later, to react against repressive violence. This seems to suggest that those of our values that epitomise the harmonious and creative civil society – peace, justice, human rights and respect for life – are a collective possession, possibly a facet of shared mind, rather than merely individual ideals. It may be plausible to think of them as constituting the heart of a fully human system. If so, like our human potentials, they are always available.

Following these men, many others have explored the implications of their views. James Lovelock, for example, advanced the concept of the universality of mind towards the idea that our planet was a sentient living creature capable of adjusting temperature, climate, etc according to need. This was of course the so-called Gaia hypothesis, derided by some and uncritically lauded by others, but which many serious scientists came to feel to be significant, though in need of some redefinition.

Psychological insights – Freud, Jung, Wilber

Naturally the whole area was of great interest to psychologists. The psychiatrist Carl Gustav Jung, who broke away from his deterministic mentor, Sigmund Freud, held there to be a collective unconscious shared by all humans, a great repository of humankind's myths and fantasies as well as the shadows of a pre-mammalian past. He wrote that 'The collective unconscious is common to all; it is the foundation of what the ancients called "The sympathy of all things"'. In this respect Jung's particular torch has passed to transpersonal psychology, a somewhat wider set of concepts about 'extended mind' and in general our shared mental life. The different approaches of these schools have been integrated in the work of Ken Wilber. He posits various levels of consciousness, ranging from the interpersonal through the bio-social and the communal, to the cosmic. Wilber refers to this consciousness as Mind.

Implications for society

The work of Prigogine, Bateson, Wilber and other respected scientists and scholars, though not specifically much concerned with peace, social change, violence and so on, nevertheless signposts the route we must travel to affect the Hydra. That is to say, to bring about changes of perception, *changes of heart*, on a scale sufficiently massive to influence *systems*.

The Gaia hypothesis may be incorrect, but even if our planet is not a systemic organism, it is the host to an infinity of lesser overlapping ecological subsystems. We humans are involved in a vast number of these systems as well as others, social in character, to do with politics, religion, education, etc – matters on which there is a considerable amount of choice; in this, social systems differ from those of simple organisms, which do not.

Mind, in Bateson's sense, characterises all living systems. But within the systems that comprise living organisms, the individual brainless parts such as molecules, have a limited reactive capacity; their behaviour is very accurately predictable. On the other hand, because of the variety and complexity of social systems and their living components, the dissipative structures are very open. This makes it very hard to generalise about them – hence, among other things, our variability in realising and then effectively adjusting our potentials to personal or social issues; we have all experienced the frustrating difficulty of applying what we (believe we) know to actual problems.

Also, of course, human beings share in, or at least have access to, a great realm of information and ideas that spur them to preserve the system, but – except in very isolated groups – not so unanimously nor so completely as to maintain it wholly unchanged. Feedback loops relating to social mores, for example, or education inculcated by one generation, do much to form the attitudes and reactions of the next one. These, however, are subject to some modification from outside influence – possibly religious or political extremism, or the impact of exceptional individuals or groups. Thus some measure of change remains possible and indeed probable. On the whole, however, social systems and structures are more prone to *evolutionary* change that preserves a recognisable basic character.

How, then, does *revolutionary* change take place in a relatively static military or highly conservative or authoritarian regime?

In fascist or other societies steeped in the culture of violence, social systems tend to become restricted and narrow, more similar to the functioning of much simpler organisms. Such a system could be said to be less human because there was less scope for individuals to develop their *truly human* capacities for wisdom, compassion, moral courage, and of course the happiness that goes with these.

These capacities are precisely the ones needed for the smooth and creative functioning of any society. The scarcity of many of them in the numerous oppressive regimes throughout the world is no doubt responsible for their defects of economy and administration, let alone of maintaining human rights and high culture.

To the extent that any society (or indeed family) is similarly dominated by the Hydra's culture of violence, it forfeits the lively intelligence and imagination of its people. It becomes less competent – consider the breakdown of the USSR. For the same reason, it becomes drab and dull if not directly unpleasant, as did Zaire under Mobutu. A more richly endowed and peaceful form of society would seem enormously desirable to all who had not been crushed or co-opted by the stultifying regime. At this point, perhaps, there comes into being a powerful collective consciousness, a unified mind-set which touches the minds of many who might hitherto have been unaffected by the situation.

Our great responsibility is to make this awareness ever more readily available. We must learn how better to withstand and to undermine the culture of violence by strengthening our minds' understanding, and in that way strengthening and stimulating the emergence of a wider and purposeful consciousness. This happened, on a large scale, in Eastern Europe in 1989.

I believe we have significant things to learn from the work so briefly and inadequately summarised in this chapter. One, just noted above, is that there is probably some kind of collective awareness, extended mind, or whatever we may call it, that has an enormously powerful – but often unacknowledged – impact on human feeling and action. The question of how this can be mobilised to promote the taming of the Hydra, the culture of peace and the pursuit of happiness will be discussed later.

A second thing is that in social systems there is a positive correlation between greater dissipative efficiency, openness, tensile strength, competent self-regulation, and conditions that are favourable to development of human potential. And it is encouraging that this appears to be in closer conformity with general 'natural' principles than more rigid social systems in which these qualities are weak. Indeed, that what scientific findings have suggested to be the normal, or in a sense 'healthy', conditions of objects alive or even inanimate which are accessible for analysis, are so far as is possible to judge, comparable with what we would consider the good, 'healthy' society.

And the third point is that social systems are, so to speak, pervaded with mind; the two are interdependent. The implications for eroding the culture of violence and promoting the culture of peace and the pursuit of happiness are enormous. They emphasise the need for holistic thinking, and stress the caution with which we view any slick answer to the 'problem of violence'. I trust that the practical examples given in the next chapter will clarify these points.

We must also bear in mind that the holism just mentioned includes the fact that all societies are a plaid of interwoven institutions, values and attitudes. If the balance of these attitudes is changed, strange paradoxes may develop. For example, at their extremities, capitalism and communism may curl around towards each other, each being dominated by rich and powerful elites infinitely aloof from the well-being of the masses they govern. Thus the culture of violence cannot be maintained or its institutional structure developed in a *culture in which happiness has been largely recaptured.*

The extended mind

This is a topic that lends itself to rumour and falsification, an unfortunate fact because it plays a powerful, but little really understood part in our lives. Through it we are subjected to influences that we do not usually recognise as such, and no doubt ourselves exercise an unintended and perhaps indirect influence on others.

Here follow a few fairly clear examples, some personal, of the operation of the extended mind which strengthened my belief in it as a reality rather than a myth.

One phenomenon I consider to be a reality has actually been turned into a myth, perhaps because the subject of a quasi-fictional book. It is the 'legend of the hundredth monkey'. I find this to be credible because it is the subject of a chapter in a book and an article by separate Japanese scientists in reputable publications. The story is as follows: an enclosed colony of Japanese monkeys living by the coast were largely fed on potatoes. One discovered by chance that washing the vegetable made it pleasanter to eat because clean, and tastier because of the tang of salty water. Bit by bit a few other monkeys followed suit, but when a critical mass of monkeys had done so, suddenly all the rest followed them. But the most surprising thing is that at just the same time, a whole other colony of monkeys several miles up the coast and completely out of contact with the others, also did so.

A quite different example: my wife and I, with some friends, were waiting at night in a Bangkok restaurant for another friend to arrive from some distance away. Suddenly one of us said, 'John will be here very soon, I'll just go and meet him'. And in a couple of minutes he came back with John. There was no 'normal' way he could have known where John was. No one else had the slightest idea of his proximity.

Another experience made me realise the power that strong collective feeling can generate and of which even I, usually very insensitive, was aware. A few pages on I shall refer to the JVP insurrection of young Sinhalese Buddhists. This was a brutal rebellion, brought down with even greater brutality. The rivers were clogged with corpses and piles of bodies smouldered by the road sides. Whole villages were wiped out. Arriving by air in Sri Lanka on one occasion at the height of the slaughter, I was at once overwhelmed by a shroud of terror and despair. I saw no horrible sights on the long drive to Colombo; I learned no new facts. But the screams of the tortured rang in my ears and I suffered the dread and panic of the fugitives. For several days, feeling a strange and indefinable sickness, I could hardly sleep or eat. I shared in a larger consciousness, a great collective hopelessness and fear.

This was a grim way of experiencing the fact of our mental interconnectedness. It made me realise how much more we need to know about the psycho-social mechanisms by which changes of attitude, particularly over major events, come about. What, for example, motivated the apparently spontaneous uprising against Communist rule throughout Eastern Europe in 1989? Or the discovery of the whole tit population of England, within the space of a few weeks, that a good drink of cream could be had by pecking through the top of a milk bottle. Is Rupert Sheldrake's theory of morphic resonance, the memory linking creatures everywhere across space and generations, a truth rather than a fantasy? What brought about the extraordinary outpouring of grief at the death of Princess Diana?

My wife and I lived in Cambridge, Massachusetts throughout the 1960s and experienced the extraordinary changes that took place during that decade. I am both surprised and saddened that people now speak of that period as an absurd, even decadent age of extravagant behaviour, irresponsible students, hallucinogens, the beginning of the drug epidemic, and general silliness. All that is true, but it was a by-product of something much more important: *millions of people, including forty-year-olds like us, were driven to seek, and some to actually perceive a different reality*; in my case my perception of race, sex, religion, the relations of the teachers to the taught, were radically and permanently changed for – I like to think – the better, the more realistic.

And we also observed the great reversal of those trends during the next decade.

How did these shifts of awareness come about? I have read various socio-psychological explanations of this amazing phenomenon, but to one who lived through and was greatly moved by it, they were all superficial. I do not, of course, know the answer to this question, but I know it is worth asking. If we knew the answer we might transform the energies of the Hydra and rehabilitate happiness.

Unfortunately, we know more about bad influences than good ones. It is easier, for example, to understand the return to the obvious rewards of materialism in the 1970s, than to remain with the other-worldliness of the previous decade. Or the malign power of Hitler than the saintliness of Mother Teresa. Or the psychic forces of agony and terror than those of peace and mercy – or is this perhaps not true? Maybe it is just that while the latter strokes us very softly, we are bludgeoned into awareness by the former.

It is in any case sure that the spirit generated by the sustained and active love of the Osijek Centre members (discussed at length in the next chapter) and other groups of *intelligently devoted* men and women throughout the world have touched the hearts of those around them; women and men then came to share their vision of gentleness and generosity. But although it may need the energy and drive of one or two people to kick-start the enterprise, I suspect it may need a critical mass of men and women to create a communal consciousness. What I experienced in Sri Lanka was the overflowing horror of tens of thousands. What Hitler's great rallies achieved was to stimulate a collective pride, anger and sense of destiny spreading far beyond the people actually attending the rally. What Churchill's impassioned speeches and the obvious peril of England did was to create a mass feeling of confidence, determination and, strangely enough, good cheer.

What we now need is an equal sense of danger from the Hydra and of outrage against it – the wars, the injustices, the terrible weapons, the maiming of the environment, the *unnatural quality of life*. But because it gives us such a 'good time' (or could do if we were lucky), we are half-hearted and fail to generate a strong mind-set to save the situation and to restore our dwindling happiness and sense of ease.

My friend Hugh Miall, who was generous with his time to read this book in draft, asked some penetrating questions about the extended mind. These went far beyond the anecdotal justification for believing in it that I have used to back up Jung, Wilber and others. He notes that in different places I have identified it with the Gaia, with creative social movements, and with more acute awareness. This is true. However, I have not done so to make a special point; if, as I maintain, the world is a great network of interconnectedness, then *all things must be envisaged within that network.* It embraces the Hydra, and the force of the Hydra comes from the shared mind of aficionados, including people like me. It embraces the dark things and the light ones; the murderers of Rwanda and those who try to heal the wounds of war.

Hugh asks if 'the metaprogram of our culture, all the shared habits, gestures, understandings of the world which programs the young as they are socialised, and to which we all contribute, is a kind of extended mind'. I would say it probably is, at least parts of it; and am grateful for this clarification of identification.

To conclude, I would like to suggest firmly that the extended mind is NOT something extraordinary, exceptional, mystical. It is as much a part of nature as the simultaneous wheeling of a great flock of birds. As such, we can become aware of it, notice its operation in our own lives, cultivate it, and with others work to make it a conscious force for change towards a more peacefully creative civil society. To transform the Hydra to this end will require a vast educational effort, by millions of people. In order to build up the power they will necessarily need to be *aware of what they are doing, what is being done to them, and what they need to do to transform themselves and society.* The actual tools, the object lessons they will then use, will vary enormously – politics, economic changes, psychology, industrial and agricultural reform, etc., etc., etc. *But it is the mind, the spirit, in which they are used that will give them the spread and the strength.*

Having said this, however, I must move briefly into an area of which I have little direct knowledge. That is, a possible level of consciousness *beyond* what we know from the senses. My clearest possible experience of it came about in 1982 when I was listening to the Dalai Lama talking in Tibetan, of which I know not a word, but being translated into English by an Italian. As I listened, I realised when the translator had made a mistake. At the time, I accepted this without surprise. Only some while after did I realise that the Dalai Lama's mind had communicated directly with mine without the need for any intermediary.

It seemed to me that he had access to a level of consciousness and control which was higher than the telepathic level on which my other experiences had occurred. It seems to me quite possible that the power and influence of such as Mother Teresa and my friends in Osijek who are so committed to something outside themselves, may be at this same level. What, you may ask, about Hitler and other charismatic but terrible people? Well, I do not think such abilities have anything to do with morality, rather with one-pointed energy and determination. Mother Teresa and the Dalai Lama had, in addition to their natural qualities, the most rigorous mental training directed towards the development and active expression of love and compassion. So, perhaps, through force of circumstances, have many people who have worked selflessly for those in need.

Herein may be an important lesson for those hoping to transform the Hydra.

Isn't it a really lousy life,
so much to worry over –
mad cow disease, irradiation,
salmonella and – my God –
inflation and the bloody interest rate.
I really can't enjoy things properly,
my Caribbean cruise was nearly spoilt
by queasiness of Wall Street.
So turn on the telly,
but its not much help –
slaughter in Beirut
or Sarajevo, famine in Sudan,
hear about Islamic Jehad,
Sendero Luminoso, the massacre of Kurds,
eliminated Amazonian tribes,
Saddam Hussein, Pol Pot, the rest,
global warming and pollution
Makes you mad, doesn't it,
this senseless rage and careless greed,
fanatical self-righteousness –
good that we aren't like that.

So try another channel,
let's look at something cheerful
for a change, some nice comic
to take our mind off things.

7

Principle and practice

In this chapter I shall discuss examples or practical implications of the principles just considered. I take as examples several types of Hydra-taming/peace-making activities which I know about, having been directly involved with them.

First, however, I should emphasise that underlying the specific issues and methods to be discussed, is the question of order. The reliability of national and international institutions, the probity of banks and businesses, the integrity of justice, the acceptance of responsible citizenship, democratic government – these form the essential framework for taming the Hydra. None of what we are to consider in this chapter can have any lasting effect unless it helps to create or restore these essential qualities of order. Certainly the existing economic turmoil, joint product of *dis*order and greed, would continue.

But the right order is something to which all can contribute in our daily lives, both public and private.

Education

The chief and least specific of these activities is education. I put it like this, because although I have done a good deal of university teaching, I consider education to be much wider. It could be defined as the mutual development of systems. I mean by this that *every* human contact can and ideally should be one in which all parties both teach and learn from each other, all both 'lead out' and convey something that helps to develop the potential of the other.

When I began to teach, I saw my task quite differently. My students were empty of what I felt they should be filled with; to fill them was my duty. And the more accurately they assimilated and regurgitated what I had to impart, the 'better' they were. However, when I had been touched by the spirit of the sixties, I realised that, to the extent that I had been successful, I had enslaved them. Moreover, I was doing myself an injury by separating myself from them, by not recognising and gaining from our *interbeing*.

My whole approach to teaching changed. I felt that my job was to share with them, to learn from them, and to respond as constructively as I could to what I had learned. I no longer wanted them to caress my ego by parroting my ideas and reproducing them in the approved format of notes, references, etc. I gave up attempting to mark or grade their essays – it wasn't for me to establish hierarchies of 'good, bad, or indifferent' in terms of some subjective personal criterion of merit. I asked them instead to write or speak about what interested them in what seemed to them the most effective way. When they had done that we could discuss and learn whatever there was to be learned.

At first the students were very wary, suspecting that this was some crafty academic trick to test them, to catch them off their guard. After a while, however, they realised that I was sincere. The quality of their essays and their arguments then changed greatly. They had lost superficial polish, but they had gained amazingly in imagination, creativity, and interest.

When I commented on this they said that my approach had freed them from a stultifying convention. Previously they had always produced work designed to please the professor; now they were writing to please themselves.

And also they now pleased the professor! Our relationship helped me to invaluable insights about myself, the people I met and the situations we were involved with.

Most of the work described in the rest of this chapter involves a certain amount of the sort of education just described. The setting was not, of course, academic, but its degree of effectiveness depended largely on the amount of real sharing and exchange among the people involved. To the extent that those involved, either as allies or protagonists, solved their problems or reached agreement, there was an element of education in their relationship; *they treated each other respectfully as human beings and so learned from each other what needed to be done, and did it.*

This is the reason why the final chapters of this short book emphasise education as the central element in taming the Hydra.

Centre for Peace, Nonviolence and Human Rights, Osijek, Croatia

Osijek was violently bombarded by Serb forces from the early summer of 1991 until new year 1992 and then less ferociously until May. However, Serb occupation (though under UN administration) of the land on three sides of the town remained until January 1998. It then reverted to Croatian control. Osijek suffered severely during the war There were over eleven thousand killed and wounded and scarcely a house was left without pockmarks of shell or shrapnel.

The people were very angry and many were obsessed by the longing for revenge; anyone who spoke about peace was branded a traitor. They were not satisfied with the UN-maintained cease-fire and longed for the chance to drive the Serbs out.

Two people, however, thought differently. A woman, Katarina Kruhonja, a physician, and a political scientist, Krunoslav Sukic got to know each other and shared their distaste for the hate-filled mood of aggression. They decided to start an organisation to promote peace education based on nonviolence (a new concept for them) and human rights. Few people were interested; most were hostile. However, they decided to go ahead and launch the idea with a series of lectures and public discussions, which I had the good fortune to attend. The reception was luke-warm but polite.

At this stage there were, besides Katarina and Kruno, only four or five individuals who wanted to explore the ideas of peace and nonviolence any further.

These people, however, impressed me greatly and I returned after a few weeks for further discussions. Katarina and Kruno had organised a workshop and invited about twenty women and men who were concerned over peace issues to attend. The meeting lasting five days.

We met in rather unsuitable borrowed rooms and talked and talked. The main topics were our nature and its potentials; what held these back; how they could be developed; and how they might be applied to the problems of violence and anger in Osijek. It was very significant that half-way through the workshop, the participants, some of whom had not previously met, began to talk in a different manner. Hitherto they had spoken as though the problems we were discussing were only objectively interesting, matters of academic rather than practical concern.

Now, however, they had become involved, speaking of 'we' rather than 'I' – what shall *we* do, how shall *we* arrange the meetings, *who* will take notes, etc. The Centre was no longer the idea of a couple of people; it was becoming an organism.

Now, seven years later, what was a tiny group meeting informally in temporary accommodation, has 50 members and altogether 135 people involved with the various active projects that have been set up. These are to do with education, psychosocial support of refugees and displaced persons of whom there have been tens of thousands, liaison with and support for other peace groups in other former Yugoslav countries as well as Croatia, and human rights on which three lawyers are working. In all its work and contacts it strives to build and maintain the nucleus of the civil society resistant to any kinds of divisions – ethnic, religious, political or ideological – imposed by the violence of war or by pressure within the surrounding society.

The work on human rights has perhaps been the anvil on which the spirit of the Centre has been forged. In the early stages of the Centre powerful local figures were evicting people from government housing if they had the slightest connection with Serbia – for example if a woman's husband had served in the predominantly Serbian former Yugoslav army. This was illegal, but in the prevailing atmosphere, nobody cared. Centre members would wait in the apartments of people who had been told they must move, ready to confront and argue with the armed men who come to carry out the eviction.

After a particularly unpleasant episode in which people were beaten, Katarina and Kruno went in protest to the high official concerned. Far from apologising, however, he issued a barbarous but horridly plausible threat to have them killed if they continued this work. This provoked tense debate among the Centre members, but they decided that though they might modify their techniques and enlist more help from local clergy and lawyers, they must continue as before; to do otherwise would take the moral guts out of all their work.

Not long after, when I commented on their cheerful and lighthearted mood they answered that when they had firmly made up their minds to ignore the threats, they felt liberated.

Equally central to the Centre's work is members' concept of nonviolence. To some this mainly means doing without violence what is usually done by use of it. Katarina's interpretation of nonviolence leads her, in all her contacts, including those with people who are hostile to her, to try to serve them. Whatever she says or does, aims to help them to overcome fear or hatred or whatever it may be that is impeding the development of their potential as complete human beings.

Every two years the Centre holds a 'Week of Peace and Culture' in which the whole town is involved – there are exhibitions, discussions, music, children's parties, and feasts. It is the occasion for the Centre to reaffirm its dedication to peace and to the people of Osijek, who attend in great and appreciative numbers. Through such activities as the Week of Peace and Culture, the human rights work and the many refugee projects, the Centre has not only become known and liked, but many people have become identified with the principles it stands for. These have, so to speak, spread into the city like a yeast, creating the ferment that could lay the foundations of a new form of society not susceptible to the fear and anger that lead to violence.

The members of the Centre, some of whom were at first anxious and uncertain, now are cheerful, sure and strong. *To work together for the well being of others appears to be a powerful way to evoke primal happiness.*

The Osijek Centar za Mir, as the Centre is called locally, exemplifies several of the characteristics referred to in the previous chapter as to be found in systems both social and natural. In particular, its growth and expansion in a hostile environment show it to be a truly dissipative structure sufficiently unstable to enable new structures to emerge – as they have done; there have been several subgroups which have grown like spores flung out by the energy of the Centre. At the same time it is stable in the sense of being flexibly adaptive, but far from being in a fixed state of equilibrium. What Prigogine and his colleagues have seen as a basic quality of *nature* emerges in Osijek as a basic quality of *social organisation*. By contrast to this, the larger society of the town is rigid and unadaptable.

From the psychological point of view and without carrying out any particular research or tests, but judging by my own friendships with Centre members and observing their relationships with others, it seems clear that they have gone some way to escape the ego-cage. That is to say, they have a more than the average sensitivity to shared consciousness or what I have termed the extended mind. I don't mean by this anything that might be termed magical or mystical, merely a faculty which we all possess, some of us to a considerable degree. A common example is the sensitivity of a long married couple to each other's feelings, to each other's very *being*.

The work of Katrina and the Centre was recognised in 1998 by the award (shared with another Croatian, Vesna Terselic, for comparable work) of the Right Livelihood Foundation, generally known as the alternative Nobel Peace Prize. This is usually given less to people involved with situations much in the public eye, such as Northern Ireland or the Middle East, than to people active with human rights, refugees and other victims of war, environmental destruction, and resistance to injustice or tyranny.

Training workshops

The difference between the Osijek Centre and others like it, and workshops, is that while the former is an organisation lasting an indefinite period of time, a workshop is a group of individuals brought together for a specific period like a week, and afterwards dispersing. The aim of most workshops is 'training'. The focus of the training may be for mediation, nonviolent action, work on human rights, or any comparable purpose. Generally, however, the underlying purpose is for the unveiling of the human potential of the participants so that they may cope more effectively with the situations they face. My friend Diana Francis is a past mistress (if this is a legitimate phrase) of the skill of training; what I know of it – and much else – is gleaned from her, Margareta Ingelstam and Scilla Elworthy who have all, in different ways, made enormous contributions to the art of peace making.

The presiding trainer or facilitator is skilled in stimulating a creative atmosphere in which the members of the group feel sufficiently supported and upheld by each other to talk freely, or weep, or express any other emotion. In this milieu of mutual help and support, the workshop normally has the same sort of value as the Centre does for its members.

In general two types of learning occur. One is that the group members will probably learn practical skills, such as mediation. More importantly, they learn about themselves and gain confidence in their capacities. They will be led, as the members of the Osijek Centre are led, by their shared concern for the well-being of others, to discover that they have unexpected strengths. We are held back by fear, ignorance, diffidence, modesty, from allowing our true capabilities to be revealed. Thus shyness is irrelevant. We are not boastful in revealing our capacities because they are not things we have acquired by our own efforts, like university degrees. They are a given part of us, and failure to express them insults our nature. Gandhi referred to the use of these abilities as *Satyagraha,* or *Truth Force*, claiming it was the most powerful force in the world, and indeed with it he brought about the most amazing changes. The great function of many workshops is to nurture the Truth Force through working together with wise facilitation.

In some cases the members of the workshop are a team, working together in any case, but it more usual for them all to separate when it is over. The disadvantage of this, from the point of view of work on the Hydra, is that they cannot generate the same collective strength as do the members of a permanent group, such as the Centre. The contradictory advantage is that they may be able to initiate valuable work in a number of other places, building up other foci of effective effort.

So far as I know, there has been no long term evaluation of workshops. Indeed because of their diversity and usually short duration it would be very difficult to make a significant assessment. From what I know, however, from attendance at and facilitation of workshops, the same principles would apply as we have discussed in relation to Osijek.

Counselling and resettlement

At the end of World War II a number of senior British army officers who had been prisoners of war in World War I told the War Office (as the now Defence Ministry was called) that their lives had been ruined by the experience of long captivity. They urged that some provision must be made for the tens of thousands of British prisoners who would be returning to England, mostly from Germany.

Soon after they came back it became clear that many of them needed some help. They had troubles with their family relations, with returning to work; they were depressed, in bad health and generally miserable.

After much discussion with psychiatrists and psychologists who had served in the army a number of what were called Civil Resettlement Units (CRUs) were set up. The word resettlement was used instead of rehabilitation to avoid the stigma of any implication of neurosis or mental illness. This would not, in any case, have been true; the men were suffering from the strain of prolonged and unpleasant captivity, absence from normal human and family relations, fear for their families of whom many had been in bombed cities, guilt at having been captured, the strangeness of the regulation-dominated post-war world.

The camps provided a stable and comprehensible army base, but one lacking compulsion and any rigid discipline, from which to get reacquainted with civilian life. Their health problems were dealt with, they were steered through the maze of rationing and other new post-war phenomena, local firms gave them opportunities to try out different types of employment. Every week-end they were given a free pass to go home, but without the worry of wondering how they were going to cope with a life from which they were to some extent estranged.

In the CRUs there were psychiatrists whom they could consult if they wanted and they met regularly for group discussions presided over by an officer. This was in the early days of group work. No one knew much about it, but in the 'safe' atmosphere of the CRUs, the men felt free to speak about feelings and experiences that had been bottled up inside them and had impeded the resumption of close relations with wives, parents and other intimates.

I was the research officer for the CRUs, and my work showed that the men who had attended the camps – there was no compulsion to do so – had re-established themselves in civilian life far more easily than those who had not. Moreover, by comparison with men who had been in reserved occupations and had never been in the army let alone been captured, they seemed to be better adjusted, healthier and happier. (Ironically, although the project had been stimulated by generals and other senior officers, very few officer prisoners of war volunteered for the CRUs; they appeared to feel that it was below their dignity to recognise they had in any sense suffered emotionally from their captivity.)

Violence and alienation

Since World War II vast numbers of women and men throughout the world have suffered worse war-traumas than the British soldiers who volunteered for the CRUs. In Bosnia, for example, almost everyone taken prisoner by Serbs, Croats or Muslim Bosniacs was tortured in a most degrading fashion. If we add to these the maimed and homeless, the refugees and the bereaved, we must recognise an unbearable weight of human suffering and loss of hope and happiness. But what is being done to relieve this pain? Good and altruistic women and men, and generous organisations such as the Red Cross and UNHCR, do what they can. But year by year fresh outbreaks of violence cause fresh trauma, and old traumas fester in the human heart, increasing the burden of the world's pain.

Here we have to recognise a terrible global vicious circle. It is a psychiatric dictum that pain breeds violence, if not directly, then indirectly. Children who have been abused are more likely than those who have not, to abuse their own children; and if they do not, to be insecure and unhappy and so unable to contribute fully to a peaceful and harmonious society. The more we react to violence with violence, the greater the volume of violence, and so it goes on and on… On the larger scale I have little doubt that the cruelty of the Croats in World War II was a powerful factor in Serb violence the next time around. And now recent reciprocal brutalities are likely to lead to further cruelties in the future; unless the repetitive cycle can somehow be broken.

A few years ago my wife and I visited two neighbouring towns, one in Bosnia and one across the river Sava in Croatia, that were suffering, and had suffered for four years of the war, from shelling. A group we were working with told us that they desperately needed some assistance in helping the very many people, particularly the young ones, who were suffering from this ordeal – there was a high rate of suicide, much anxiety and depression, panic attacks, loss of concentration.

We managed to arrange for a small group of trained counsellors (including our daughter) to give courses. These went well for the next two years, and the local people are now confident that they can continue the work satisfactorily on their own.

This, of course, is only a minute drop in an ocean of need, but the principle is good. The tangle of pain, fear and guilt after trauma may congeal within the mind, destroying the happiness of countless individuals and affecting all around them. If this is widespread, as in Germany after World War I, the agony of the war, the shock of defeat, and the subsequent wretched period of deprivation may create a national mood of shame, anger and frustration. This is a fertile soil for the growth of social sickness such as fascism.

For this reason it is a matter of the greatest importance, for the relief of individual suffering and the greater good of the community or nation, to find ways of dismantling the desperation. A general mood of defiance or despair is unreceptive, hostile and easily moved to aggression, limiting the growth of human potential to narrow material competence. Sometimes not even that, because negative emotions such as brooding worry and self-pity drain away human energy.

This delicate work of restoring the pained mind to health is most essential at the social as well as the individual level, but it is important to remember that victims of war are not suffering from psychological *illness*. Those who have lost their families or homes, endured concentration camps, seen appalling happenings, been tortured, been deprived of the most elemental human rights, are in inner agony. All those things that had made life bearable, let alone happy, have been torn from them. The only therapy for the great majority is restoration of some semblance of what they have lost, some care, a measure of security, unobtrusive sympathy, friendship.

It is also important to remember that the work of restoration should be carried out within the context of the local society. Different cultures have evolved their own approaches to healing; the therapies of other places should not be crudely applied.

These are matters of great importance and urgency. During the past decades many millions of women, men and children have suffered the emotional wounds of war, and very many of these are as yet unhealed, spreading the infection of pain and anger to future generations. This is a global problem transcending the capacity of individual communities, even nations, to deal with.

Urbane bureaucrat, tight-lipped tight-assed simulacrum of a man
ordering humanity by the standards of Whitehall and Wimbledon,
pawning your heart for the price of a bowler hat,
how serious your study of the regulations (and their political
implications) applying to aliens (undesirable) and immigrants
(illegal)
how pure your existential joy in completing the deportation
order to consign some lesser being, certainly foreign, probably
black, to torture, detention camp or some comparable form of
extinction.
Loosen those lips, that sphincter, redeem that heart. Imagine with the
inner eye opened, the multitude of refugees.
Consider:
the throngs of dispossessed criss-crossing each other's trails
throughout the world, the ravening hunters ever closing in
with yelps of pleasure to drag them from their rickety shelters,
to strip them, dowse them with petrol, dance around excited,
masturbating; then strike a match;
to slam them into cattle wagons, feed them with salted fish,
deny them water and dump the survivors in a deserted wilderness,
to hurl them into the bloody gob and rotting teeth of war;
and consider what they fled from:
the cold appraisal of the secret police, the rule of tyrants, the hatred
aroused by being just what they are, the routine of torture;
and consider kindly their hope:
for what you fine fellows have always taken for granted –
not of course for central heating, package holidays, new cars, luxurious
meals, but enough to eat, basic medicine, freedom to say more or less
what they want and to do more or less what they like;
to have, without frills, expectancy of a normal life.

Mediation

To start with, I should explain that much, but not all, of the work I shall refer to in this section was carried out under Quaker auspices and of course owes much to the wisdom and experience of my colleagues.

Mediation is aphoristically defined by the title of a book I wrote some years ago, *In The Middle*. Mediators are in the middle between the protagonists and also in the middle of the conflict between them. I should make it clear at the outset that I am not talking about mediation as it is frequently described – the dash of a Kissinger from one capital to another, wheeling and dealing, issuing threats and promises, sticks and carrots, and concluding by unleashing the B52s. This is not mediation, but arm-twisting to the point that you twist the arm right off if you don't obtain what your masters want. No, I am talking about women and men who may be citizens of some country without ambition for world leadership, or members of some church or humanitarian group which is *tout court* concerned to make peace and diminish suffering.

Their main task is to persuade the feuding parties to meet for serious discussion of their quarrel, and of how to extract themselves from it without unacceptable loss of honour or advantage, whether strategic, economic or political. (I stress that the talks must be serious, because sometimes a leader agrees to meet feeling that a show of peaceful intentions will confer some political advantage.) Not all quarrels, it should be understood, are mediable: if one or both parties want to go on fighting, either strongly believing that they might win, or desperately fearing the possibility of losing; or because the situation is so chaotic or the leadership so unstable that there are no clear positions to discuss. The best time to arrange potentially fruitful mediation is often when there is a complete military stalemate. But of course the two parties must really want peace and be prepared to make some concessions. Without the help of mediators, however, they may be afraid of doing so lest the other side consider this a sign of weakness, and renew its attack with greater ferocity.

The task of mediators is to reassure, unravel, explain and interpret, but not to advise. If asked to do so, they should only analyse the situation without judgement, saying that in their opinion there are x choices and that each of these has y implications: it is up to the protagonists to decide which is best for themselves. Mediators have no right to promote an opinion on how another nation or group should decide its future. It is a difficult job, sometimes a dangerous one. This is because even if the leaders agree with what they are doing to bring the conflict to an end, there are often more radical men in the second echelon who want the struggle to continue. They may then murder the mediators thinking they are weakening the will of the leader to go for all out victory.

It is also very difficult always to avoid occasional unpopularity with the leaders. A salient reason for this, is that paradoxically the better the leader's relationship is with the mediators, the more he is worried that they must have a comparable relationship with his enemy, the leader of the other side. If the mediator is my friend, they think, how can he also be friendly with the man I hate most? So perhaps his show of friendship with me is a sham! There is no simple solution to this problem. It can only be minimised, with luck, by consistent and sensitive good will.

The core of the mediators' work is psychological: to change the protagonists' perceptions of their opponent, of themselves and of the conflict.

The first of these requires tact. If you try to explain that he is really not the monster portrayed by the local press, but a man with decent human instincts – like you, Your Excellency – he will probably be furious. A rather extreme reaction here illustrates a common feature of the psychopathology of embattled leaders:

They are under great strain, often suspicious, angry and full of guilt for the slaughter for which they are responsible. In the attempt to get rid of these disturbing emotions, they project them onto their enemy – he's the one, it's all his fault, the bastard! Unless mediators are very careful, they will be felt as removing a psychological prop against their own, the leader's, sense of badness. The only antidote mediators can offer is support and friendship, often lacking at the top; the fear of a coup, of traitors, that one's staff and generals are not telling the truth, are plotting to take over …

So the leader, besieged by incipient paranoia (which is by no means always so unreasonable!) must be helped to see himself – or occasionally herself – as being, like his opposite number, a decent member of the human race. Again, this is to be achieved through friendship. I would stress that this must be genuinely felt; friendship cannot be successfully feigned. Mediators must therefore jettison preconceptions and snap judgements. They must make every effort to live in the same mental space as the other human being they are dealing with, to share each other's humanity.

It is to be hoped that the relationship of mediator and leader will somewhat alleviate the burden of strain and isolation (the top is a lonely and frightening place in times of war). In this perhaps slightly less stressful atmosphere he may be able to see the situation more rationally and more humanely. What is the fighting really about? Is it truly for the good of the country that young men should be killed? What price pride and honour; what do they contribute to the happiness and well-being of the people; are they worth fighting for?

The next question is: Does this sort of mediation work? There is no simple answer. The mediators meet and learn much from large numbers of people in all walks of life from presidents to manual workers, to professional people, journalists, civil servants and clergy, but they mainly *work* with decision makers. These are usually people of ability operating under pressure, whom the mediators hope to help find a way out of the trap of violence. Their responsibilities naturally are apt to make them sensitive and touchy.

Such people may of course make a wise and humane decision to seek a way to peace rather than to blunder violently ahead. This however does not mean that the mass of the people, perhaps prejudiced by years of disparaging criticism of the 'enemy', or even having genuine grounds for disliking them, will make the change of heart on which a stable peace may depend. So leaders may sometimes shy away from the peace they really want for wrong reasons of domestic politics. In such cases the role of the mediator shifts away from being between the protagonists, to being between the leader and his or her people.

A comparable difficulty occurs with cease-fires, which are not uncommonly considered by the protagonists or suggested by UN or other officials. Mediators may be called on to discuss the idea by a leader. S/he is to some extent attracted by the possibility, but is highly suspicious of the enemy leader/general: it could be a trap, he might use the lull to strengthen his defences, bring up fresh troops, he might in one way or another cheat – so, unfortunately, perhaps on the whole, better not. And it is difficult, such suspicions are not entirely paranoid. (Even if the cease-fire is agreed on the condition that it is monitored, the very monitoring, in my experience, may be rigged by one side in its favour.)

On the other hand, a cease-fire may allow tempers to cool and prejudices to subside. So why not give it a second thought?

These are agonising decisions, but whichever way they go, it is not very probable that the widespread and deep-seated involvements and interests, strategic and/or military, of the Hydra components will be greatly or lastingly affected. This sort of mediation may be one of the *Tools For Transformation* (the title of another book on mediation), but not one to which I would now give the priority that I did when I wrote it; the social and political context of most large-scale modern conflicts is often too chaotic and disordered for either mediation, negotiation, or military planning. However, even if mediation is not practicable in many contemporary wars, the *basic* methods and approaches considered here are valid in less desperate circumstances, especially in the context of the community, the school, or the family.

Moreover, should the global situation become more orderly, effective mediation may be more readily practised. It may, therefore, be of use to consider some practical experiences.

One of my most demanding experiences of mediation was in the Nigerian civil war, mainly known as the Biafran War, of 1967-1970. It started with terrible massacres and before long Eastern Nigeria, calling itself Biafra and seeking separation from Federal Nigeria, was cut off from communication with the rest of the world, a starving and tormented enclave. Not long after the start of hostilities it could only be reached by relief planes (and mediators) after difficult flights in complete darkness, without the use of radio, and landing on a specially widened road.

On two occasions, we (there were three of us and we usually travelled in pairs) came very close to securing a cease-fire, but both times a change of fortune on the battle field led one side to go on fighting – after all, they thought, maybe they had a chance of winning or at least of getting better terms.

We had a very close and honest relationship with the Federal Nigerian leader, a most intelligent, thoughtful and decent young general, and a number of the leading Biafrans whom we respected, but we were not so close to the Biafran leader, also a military man. Over the whole period we had profound discussions with most of these men in sincere attempts to find some way in which their differences could be harmonised, trying to explain to each side the feelings of their opponents.

Very early in 1970 I had a telephone call from the then Secretary General of the Commonwealth, saying he had just had news that there had been an unexpected breakthrough by the Federal troops and that the war was expected to be over in a few days: would I go to Nigeria as soon as possible; since I knew the leadership on both sides I might be able to prevent another bloodbath like those with which it had begun?

I went with great foreboding, not knowing what I could do and expecting a scene of violent chaotic destruction. But I was completely wrong. The war had ended in an almost miraculous mood of reconciliation in which the victorious soldiers, instead of butchering their defeated enemies treated them like brothers, gave them their own rations, gave them money, took the wounded to hospital. Neither were there any reprisals at a higher level. Any 'Biafran' who had held a Federal appointment, such as ambassador, before the struggle, was at once reinstated on full pay.

How did this happen? We were told by some who were in a position to make a sound judgement that it was partly the result of work by people like ourselves, who were constantly striving for sympathetic mutual understanding, and attempting to correct inaccurate and hostile propaganda. (For example, it was quite clear towards the end of the war that the ferocity of the Biafrans' resistance was due much less to callous bloodthirstiness than to fear of what might happen if they lost.) Being able to move (though with considerable physical difficulty) between the two sides, we were in a position to give a picture unblurred by prejudice. Our views had, we were told, affected the Nigerian Federal leadership and had been successfully transmitted to the commanders in the field. But how many other influences had been at work?

If true, this was another example of the importance of the extended mind and transpersonal relationships. We found this also in another African war, the Zimbabwean independence struggle.

Quakers had been involved in this issue for many years, but I can only speak personally about the last two years of the struggle, 1978-1980. In that period we (four of us this time, but again travelling in pairs) moved constantly around the whole area – to what was then Rhodesia itself; to Mozambique, where one wing of the Patriotic Front (Mugabe's) was based; to Zambia, where the other wing (Nkomo's), was based; to Botswana, one of the other front line states; to Tanzania, which was another of them, and especially important as the president, Julius Nyerere, was the chair of the Front Line States Committee; and to South Africa, which of course was deeply and dishonourably embroiled in the whole affair. And finally we were in London for the Lancaster House talks where the settlement was eventually agreed.

Our role was comparable to that in Nigeria, but more complex and perhaps more nebulous. At the end, however, the leading figure of our group had letters from two of the involved African presidents we had come to know. They thanked us for having kept alive their hope for a peaceful solution. In Northern Ireland, recently so much anxiously in our minds, I spent four years of frequent week-end visits and a number of longer stays; much of this was fruitless except that I made a number of friends (which of course is always fruitful). But during the last years I worked with an imaginative and resourceful Irishman. He believed that if the Catholic and Protestant paramilitaries could work together on matters of common concern – housing, jobs, social services, the future for their children – they would discover that the significance of these transcended political and religious differences. These were men who were respected much more than the political leaders, for whom there was then general contempt. If the paramilitaries could take over aspects of local government, demonstrating that they were capable of responsible citizenship, the British government might dilute the control of Westminster and reduce the army presence. They were cautiously interested in the idea.

Quiet meetings were arranged in remote places and were remarkably successful. The 'hard men', who knew all about one another, but had never seen each other except through the sights of an armalite rifle, drank and sang together and found that they really liked each other!

But it all went wrong. One of the meetings was discovered by the press. In the subsequent ructions a prominent Protestant was shot (by Protestants, actually, such was the ambiguity). And the Northern Ireland Secretary was promoted and succeeded by a man who had entirely different ideas and immediately cut off all contact with what he called terrorists. This again led to a number of assassinations. I realised there was nothing I could usefully do for some time and became involved with violence in another land.

Lastly, I will say something about an awful but fascinating episode in Sri Lanka – not the Tamil war with which I was concerned for the second half of the 1980s and which was temporarily in abeyance, but the insurrection of the Janatha Vimukti Peramuna (People's Liberation Front – JVP) which I have referred to earlier. This was a Marxist movement of young Sinhalese desperate at the limits of economic opportunity. The JVP waged a brutal campaign, but the government responded with even more ferocious and indiscriminate slaughter. At the height of the massacre I got to know the president, who was deeply concerned by the killings and was convinced that if he could meet the JVP leadership, they could come to a mutually satisfactory agreement. But the urgency was great. The intelligence and the military were desperately trying to hunt down the leader, Rohana Wijewira. If they caught him, he would be killed and the JVP destroyed as an organisation. There would then be no chance for its members to be absorbed as democratic citizens into society. The resentment would smoulder underground.

My colleagues working in Sri Lanka already had contact with a small group of young people who seemed to have some links with the movement. (I should explain that the JVP were very secretive. The members belonged to quite small cells and never saw who gave them instructions. There were, I think, five tiers through which a message had to pass from the bottom level to reach the top.)

The president told us what concessions he could make to satisfy the JVP demands. This we transmitted to our JVP group; subsequently we took their response to the president; and so on, back and forth until there seemed to be a full basis for agreement. All that remained then was the problem of bringing the JVP leadership to meet the president without them being seized on the way and then certainly killed...

But we were too late. Wijewira was found, living with his wife and five children like a landed gentleman on his tea estate. He was taken with his deputy to Colombo where they were both killed almost immediately 'while trying to escape'. The young spokesman of our JVP group disappeared, presumably having also been tortured and killed. We were afraid we might have been to blame for the inadequate security of our meetings, but in fact one of the intelligence officers had by chance recognised him from a photograph. The insurrection was over, as was the cease-fire with the Tamil Tigers. A few years later the president was blown to pieces, together with twenty-three others – including the Tamil suicide bomber.

I have been involved in other conflicts and other mediations in Asia and Europe and, to a small extent, in America, but I think that the ones I have described offer a reasonable sample of the variety of situations that can arise. How should we assess them?

They do not represent, as I once thought with youthful (although I was old enough to know better) enthusiasm, the sovereign remedy for our troubles, but a means of tackling only particular aspects of them. The subsequent tyranny in Nigeria and corruption in Zimbabwe, both show that the end of the war doesn't bring the real peace. It is only a step in the right direction. The continuing plotting and sporadic violence in Ireland and further wars between India and Pakistan all show how frail, in the wide embrace of the Hydra, are the forces of harmony, tolerance and forgiveness.

Other people can tell other stories and some of them are happier. Wars do come to an end. Depressions do turn (sometimes) into booms – though the gain may be illusory. We have to recognise the facts of impermanence and to remember that what we consider 'good' things and times alternate with 'bad' things and times.

However, if we are aware that such judgements are more reflections of our own state of mind than of the objective qualities of what we are assessing, our life will be happier and calmer.

Conclusion

I return again to the concept of the Hydra. So far it is stronger than the armies of peace – consider examples of our failures: the Middle East, the Great Lakes area of Africa, the Caucasus, Sierra Leone, the Gulf, Bosnia (though there perhaps the jury is still out).

We have had some successes. The very existence of the United Nations is one. We have prevented violence in some places and restored normality in others. But these are often no more than the lancing of boils. The infection that caused them remains. I believe, however, that some of the approaches I have outlined have had more than an immediate practical value: they may have had a transforming impact which will last beyond their more superficial purpose of stopping the killing. Such, perhaps, were the great educational efforts made by the allies after World War II in Japan and in Germany, where I am happy to have had the chance to play a minuscule part. But can we say that the Hydra is now dormant in those parts?

I also believe that the scientists of mind and system have divined certain universal principles which I have recognised in my own experience, but though we may be on the right track we are still largely ignorant of our own nature, the psychological forces that dominate society and – especially, of course, the power of the Hydra.

Later we will consider a more profound means of transforming the Hydra's power (or at least reducing it), of neutralising the poison in the boil of violence and restoring some of our mutilated happiness.

8

Summary

Before moving on to a strategy for defusing our violent situation and changing the culture of violence which has come to dominate the world, we can draw together the different strands we have been discussing.

One of the main strands is, of course, the Hydra itself. This, as we have considered, is an interwoven tangle of forces, often mutually hostile but congruent in acting with political, economic or military violence in their pursuit of their own aims. Their purpose is basically profit – for themselves, or their shareholders or supporters, which really means the same thing. But this purpose is largely mindless and automatic; we react like machines. Those who oppose this blind purpose they (and in a sense, we) crush by one means or another.

These forces are often sustained by an unquestioned quasi-religious doctrine. This has occasionally a more or less conventionally religious character, but is more likely to be some political ideology – in certain places still the remains of communism, or pseudo-democracy (opponents being automatically branded anti-democratic), the market, some fabricated cult such as racial purity, or the cosmetic illusion of working charitably for the benefit of the poor (I fear that the development work in which I was involved for several years was largely of this sort).

But millions of people – most of the rich in the G7P countries, with their clients, agents and representatives in the poor ones – get some spin-off from the collective wealth of the Hydra. Even if they don't actively support it or participate in its activities, they share by osmosis much of its outlook and morality. Usually without fully realising the fact, they are accomplices in the execution of violent acts. The acceptance of violence in the schools, in the prisons, the homes, on the television, above all in the minds of most of us, represents the hidden core of the worldwide culture of violence richly nourished by the Hydra, particularly in the globalisation of the last decades. *Even the majority who gain absolutely nothing from the Hydra, who are indeed ground down by it, are profoundly influenced by their longing for what it offers: they and we, the more prosperous, are BOTH a part of the Hydra.*

The second great theme is happiness. Where there is violence, joy is tarnished and broken. Where there is no happiness, violence flourishes. But happiness is not weak; it is an essential quality of living beings. If it can survive the batterings of physical and psychological events, it is a powerful shield against the assaults of the violent mind-set. Unfortunately, however, this mind-set is particularly beguiling. It provides us with comforts, pleasures, interests, entertainments, luxuries – and the motive and justification for defending them. It supplies oblivion making us forgetful of the human and environmental cost at which they are provided. Many of these delights are trivial, adding nothing to the essentials of human well-being; contributing only to the solace of paltry desires gratified and the illusions of evanescent happiness. In these days it is rare to meet a person who is deeply and constantly happy.

But happiness is a vivid and active force, and it is not alone. It is an inseparable part of our great inner resource of wisdom, courage and compassion. If we are in a position to observe the actions of people caught up in sudden crisis, we will see amazing spontaneous acts of bravery, ingenuity and concern for others. The power of such true happiness is venom that shrivels the Hydra.

But we are alienated and confused. We can't adequately assail the Hydra until we have dealt with its shadow within ourselves. We must become aware of our own being (this is discussed in the next chapter), and explore our own minds and feelings. Part of this self-knowledge is at a deep, semi-subconscious level reached through meditative reflection rather than sharply focused thought; and part at the level of intellectual discovery and analysis that depends mainly on a process of education (again to be discussed in the next chapter): *it is essential to understand the workings of the Hydra in ourselves.*

It is equally important to understand our happiness – or lack of it. What is it that takes away our joy; what does it *feel like*? What is its connection with our hopes and fears, with our feelings about *ourselves*? This examination will reveal the extent and manner of our dependence on the Hydra, and our degree of freedom from its thrall.

I do not feel it is either necessary or desirable, in view of the great differences between individuals and their circumstances, to suggest *what* anyone should actually *do*. Virtually anything from talking to a neighbour, to travelling in a distant country on a dangerous and difficult peace mission, can be equally worthwhile. But the value depends on the degree of realisation of the facts, inner and outer, of interdependence, impermanence and the *natural power* of nonviolence.

These facts include the findings of research in psychology and the natural sciences that the openness, flexibility, and tensile strength of systems, both living and material, is essential to the creative survival of social systems.

For these reasons, the Hydra should never be admired for its ruthless efficiency and taken as a model, as many politicians have done through their belief in, even worship of, the Market. Ruthless it is, but not a model for anyone who views the flowering of the human spirit as a supreme good. If the implications of the natural world are to be taken seriously, it is a sick system which will collapse as have others such before.

But we should be encouraged by the Hydra's sickness. To the degree that we dissent from it and its culture of violence, we could be stronger than it is, and dismantle it. We could then use its tremendous energies and practical skills to build for life.

Brief note on war

I have been eager to stress the importance of interconnection as the source of all events – especially the Hydra – rather than the events themselves. This has led me to say less about war and other aspects of large-scale violence than might have been wise or expected. War, of course, is both a product of the Hydra forces and one which generates fresh forces and – as may easily be seen – further struggles, famine, abuse, injustice, tyranny. But one reason why I have said so relatively little about war is that it is so intractable. Once the violence has broken out and bloodshed and injustices have been perpetrated, implacable feelings are aroused. Once the fighting has started it is propelled by emotional forces that are almost impossible to resist, especially if rooted in the past; far better concentrate on prevention.

The work towards a reasonable settlement should ideally be begun as soon as anyone recognises the existence of a disagreement that could degenerate into an escalating quarrel. Then is the time to start what is fashionably called a 'peace process'. Even so it may be too late, as we have arguably seen in the Middle East, in South Africa torn by crime and communal violence, and – as I write – most tragically in Northern Ireland. This last instance grimly illustrates the general principle of obdurate violence. The 'peace process' was followed with meticulous skill, tact and persistence. There were some stumbles, but mostly the various parties behaved *as if* they wanted it to succeed rather than to fall apart. Hitherto the process had been followed in the light of a possible future rather than the dark of a receding past. But then came the marching season and the antique hatreds began to smoulder. The larger the crowds at Drumcree, the more intense the violence in the streets of Belfast, and the more Catholic churches burnt, the greater the possibility that the delicate work of peace building will be blown apart. The future of the peace process is in the balance. Either way, however, the lesson is clear. Never delay before attempting to unravel the sources of violence, never underestimate the power of the past. However deeply it may be slumbering in the human heart, it may awake.

Above all, however, we should so profoundly understand that we *feel with our whole being*, rather than just intellectually, the futility of war and its consequences.

Night implacable descends
stabbing the earth with frigid rain.
The hunt is up.

The fugitive is desperate on the run.
'Blood, blood', false prophets shriek,
smooth prelates sight the victim
through the murk and squeal with lust,
pterodactyls, risen from extinction,
hurtle towards the stumbling body,
plump ministers of state,
grinning and slicking back their hair,
join in the hunt.

And so do I,
and also am the prey.

As Christmas ads do not exactly ask,
what does the man with everything
give to the man with nothing?
Well, here's a new twist to the theme:
What he gives is a new social status –
outcast non-entity unperson.
What does the poor man give to the rich one – all,
an opening for charity and grace,
but needle-eyed and so ignored.

This shivering pariah
squats below the arches,
derelict waster rubbish,
a man of sorrow
acquainted with grief and the poisoned bliss
of meths and cyder, the scrapings of trash cans,
and with hunger failure and rejection.

Getting contemptuous kicks
from poverty and pain,
the wealthy passer-by
compares their lots:
his virtue recompensed with
smart suburban home and Audi;
the other's foolish weakness
repaid in currency of filth and penury.

9

Strategy for happiness

My mother, who was born in 1878 and lived to be over 90, hated God. She told me that as a young woman she was greatly depressed by the idea of this disagreeable being watching her the whole time, disapproving and judgemental. But it never occurred to her that it was possible *not* to believe in God, just as one *had* to believe in the existence of the sun. It was just there as everyone knew, like it or not.

One day, a brother whom she greatly respected told her that it was quite possible not to believe in God. A lot of people did not; they were called atheists. My mother was delighted, and at once proclaimed herself an atheist; she was very happy not to have to believe in anything so nasty as the Victorian version of the deity. Thereafter, she never went to church except for such occasions as weddings, which she loved, and she certainly never joined any religious body. But she was nevertheless what we might call a spiritual person. She loved very deeply, had faith in the goodness of people, grieved greatly at their sorrows and would do anything to help them; she had no thought or concern for herself and lived very simply for the day. It took very little, no – nothing, to make her happy; she *was* happy.

I am not saying that religious belief makes people unhappy; I know many who seriously rejoice in it. I am simply saying that it is not necessary, but that on the other hand *the capacity to love is essential to and indeed IS happiness*. A religious person would probably say that this is a naively simple faith; and this is probably true. It *is* faith, but in the basic goodness of human nature, not in God, nor the Tory Party, nor Communism, nor anything external to oneself.

My mother managed to reach this source within herself without any instruction or psychological aids. Many branches of the Christian faith do, however, have a system for so doing, especially the monastic orders; so do the Buddhists, Muslims, Hindus and Jews. And many find one of the systematic practices very helpful.

The ego

My mother, however, was a natural. But most of us are not, and have to approach, as I do, by the more fallible cerebral route.

This involves the deconstruction of the ego. Freud thought of the ego as being the part of the psychic structure which is concerned with facing up to the demands of the real world, and dealing both with the impulses from the Id and the requirements of the superego. Most people think of it, however, as something like the *Self.* When they say of someone that she has a strong ego, they mean a person with what we call character, with firm opinions, self-assured and purposeful. Someone with a weak ego is the opposite, a man or woman unsure, vacillating, diffident.

There is also a completely different meaning to ego. Here the concept of ego is not a thing in itself, but the *idea* we have of ourselves, whether weak in the sense just defined, or strong, but not the *reality*. Here the ego is not I, but a constructed identity based on mistaken ideas. It is to be eroded by watchfulness and self-observation which exposes its pretensions to be the real Mary Smith or Adam Curle.

It is an illusion that obscures the ultimate reality of our nature – our great potential for wisdom, moral courage, compassion and happiness, the *Mind*. Of the two illusions, however, the strong may be worse than the weak because of the self-satisfaction it generates and the demands it makes on others.

It is crucially important to understand these illusions if we are to take on the dual tasks of rescuing happiness by transforming the concatenation of destructive forces I refer to as the Hydra. The most significant ability we can develop as a habit (not all habits are bad unless we are not conscious of them!) is *Awareness*.

There are probably three main levels of awareness. The first is that we are conscious, but not really awake to what we are doing; for example, we may be walking, but our thoughts are entirely occupied with something, so that although we see the surrounding countryside in the sense that our eyes pass over it, we notice nothing and could not later remember anything we had 'seen'. With the second we know that we are walking along a particular road to reach a particular destination and take some note of what we have walked past. With the third we are aware what it *feels like* to be doing it and *notice* that we are noticing our surroundings. In this third level of awareness we are fully awake; in the others we are in varying degrees asleep to ourselves and our surroundings. We may recognise the third level by the brightness which seems to suffuse our surroundings. When we make the conscious effort to shift from the second to the third level, it is as though the light has been turned on.

When we are fully aware, we are aware of our true nature, acting and feeling in accordance with it; *we know who we are; we experience primal happiness.* But very few of us are fully aware for more than short periods of time. Our minds are clouded by daydreams, by anxieties, by illusions about ourselves – these constantly flicker across the screen of consciousness. It takes an awakened effort to stem their flow. I found this when I used to walk to work trying to maintain awareness of myself and my changing surroundings. Very soon, I sadly admit, I would forget what I was trying to do; my thoughts would soar far away, concerned with a television programme I had seen last night, or some quite irrelevant childhood memory, or some foolish worry.

The ego, the separate-self illusion, is both powerful and crafty. It moves smoothly and imperceptibility from one dimension to another. For example, when I hear of some tragedy, perhaps the death of a great friend, my immediate reaction springing from the source of our profound potential, is one of pure grief. I use the adjective because the feeling is untainted with any self-regard: I personify abstract sorrow. But the ego slides in: a sense of self-approbation at my depth of feeling; unhappiness for *myself* because I shall miss my friend; superiority because I was closer to and am more devastated than others by his death. Shamefully I have discarded my friend, drowned him in an ego striving for attention. Awareness is indeed hard to maintain.

But it is helpful simply to make the effort. However apparently unsuccessful, it shows that we were not powerless victims of the Hydra forces. Even if we could not avoid its economic pressures or its wars, we could escape its inner compulsions and so, in the most basic sense, be free to fight it.

A wise Tibetan, Kalu Rimpoche, has this to say about our flawed perception of reality: 'We live in a world of deluded appearances. Nevertheless, there is a reality, and we are that reality. When you understand this, you will understand that you are nothing. But being nothing, you are everything. That is all there is to it.'

The plan

What should be our strategy? *It can be summarised as Revolution through People, extending the Mind of Nonviolence until it brings about a Transformation of Practices.*

I must begin by saying that I am particularly in favour of proposals that we, even if we are *not* senior politicians or business magnates, can do something, however small, to implement. Recommendations for reforming the UN, or the World Bank, or creating vast new political, social or economic structures are frequently voiced to the great satisfaction of those who make them. But for bad, or occasionally good, reasons very few of them are listened to and still fewer acted upon. And if they are, they change and are corrupted. I hope that what I shall propose will not appear so unrealistic.

To continue in a more positive vein, I would like to say to everyone who is working in the very many spheres at all levels for peace, justice, human rights, the survival of the biosphere, in fact for the general well-being of life on the planet: Thank you, please carry on. But as you proceed with this work, bear in mind the character of the Hydra that touches all of us inwardly and outwardly; bear in mind *and study*, as already suggested, the happiness of which it so greatly deprives us; and slant your work as mediator, teacher, development worker, politician, environmentalist, judge, carer, citizen, to take account of these subtle issues. They are all connected and the strength of any specialised work will be increased if the links are understood.

But what if the destructive forces of the culture of violence are so interconnected that it appears impossible to overcome them, what is the point of all these efforts, especially since they are often *not* connected in any obvious fashion? Are not we ourselves, who wish to oppose the Hydra, also bound by the violent forces out of which it has drawn its power? Are we not caught in a cycle of economic forces affecting social attitudes, political structures affecting economic forces affecting social attitudes affecting economic forces and so on and on and on in infinite complexity? How can we hope to break into the vicious cycle of the Hydra?

Well, this is what we have been talking about all along. We are indeed trapped, but our *collective* awareness and understanding can break the Hydra's power and reverse the cycle. So let's continue, but remembering that it will be the hardest task humanity has ever faced.

Reaction and proaction

Much of the work carried out by peace and other humanitarian bodies might be described as protective, ways of minimising or guarding against damage, particularly in relation to war or post-war trauma. They are *reactive* and thus of related character to many economic, social, medical, ecological, etc. measures taken to reduce the baleful impact of the Hydra.

But it is even more crucial to think *proactively*. In order to assail the Hydra's citadel in the hearts and minds of human beings, of you and me, we all have to understand it better. It is not enough simply to vilify it, or to try – as we must – to repair the ravages it has brought about. We need to better *educate* both ourselves and others in its ways and in so doing to devise *nonviolent alternative* tactics. The work of the Osijek Centre has certainly been reactive to the mood of violent militarism, but even more *proactive* in spreading the entirely different mood of nonviolence; not just mending a broken society, but anticipating future tensions and planting the seeds of a new one.

Nonviolence, in the sense that Katarina in Osijek uses the concept – the effort in all relationships to help, to reduce fear and hatred, to bring reassurance and peace – is a proactive force for healing. In any case the change must also be psychological, within ourselves – release from an addiction to the 'real world' of the Hydra without a painful withdrawal. Violent revolutionary efforts, on the other hand, even if successful, only cut off metaphorically the Hydra's heads, without preventing the growth of replacements; violence does not solve problems, it creates new ones as history so often demonstrates – consider, for example, contemporary Congo and indeed many other parts of Africa. But the strength of nonviolence, as Gandhi knew and demonstrated by bringing down a great power, cannot be resisted – but it takes courage and insight to practise it!

Nevertheless, the Hydra's power is certainly daunting: the progressive deterioration of our precious biosphere; the economic principles and structures which are largely responsible for this as well as the growing inequalities between rich and poor; alienation; the existence and potential proliferation of nuclear and other frightful weapons; the arms trade; official injustices; drug trafficking; (no attempt is made to rank types of violence – they all feed off each other).

We know, however, as I have tried to show, that some of these can be effectively modified by groups and even individuals on a relatively small scale. Sadly, though, we are faced with a whole culture which passively accepts or tolerates these things, or grabs them avidly if it sees in them some profit or solace. In any case, we have almost all come to accept its pleasures as a matter of course – supermarkets, travel, cable TV and a vastly greater degree of sheer comfort than my generation, for example, had in our youth. To change the culture, the hearts of the assenters, active and passive, perhaps yours and mine, must also be changed; in the most accurate sense a herculean task, since their beliefs have been institutionalised within the system. We must also realise that to assail these things directly with their own weapons of violence and guile, may simply strengthen them.

I believe there is one supreme way to weaken the hold of the Hydra forces over our lives: To add to what we are already doing to oppose the forces of destruction *by informing and educating ourselves in the broadest possible sense on our situation*. This is the only way I can envisage that we may generate *the extended consciousness, the Mind force* that will affect us all. What we need, of course, is the will to give up the illusions that real happiness can come through the culture of violence. We do not need any type of initial training or to have any type of job, only to remember our humanity and the inhumanity of the Hydra system.

Public figures prance and strut
preaching the new salvation
that they've built
from pieces off the scrap heap
of economic and political ideas,
glued together with sharp practice
and deceit, painted with flattery,
polished with lies, presented by
the admen and spewed out by the media.

10

Implementation

Much of this small book is, of course, concerned with the nature of the Hydra and of happiness, and the practice of taming the former and achieving the latter. If anyone is unsure of what I have been trying to describe, I would suggest that they do some rereading before continuing with this section.

What I have written so far is comparable to the instruction manuals we are given on, say, driving a car, high jumping, fly fishing or any other activity. But as everyone knows there is a great difference between knowing what one *ought* to do and actually doing it, between knowing what one *ought* to feel or want and actually wanting or feeling it. If you think I am right in saying that (1) we ought to reduce the Hydra impulses within ourselves, (2) we could (or ought to) feel happy, and (3) we ought to share our understanding of the Hydra with others, then you will need to understand what prevents you from doing so.

This may call for a measure of analysis, not in the sense of guilty self-condemnation, but of dispassionate awareness of mental processes such as is achieved in meditation or calm reflection.

We may come to recognise the Hydra lurking in any concern for material prosperity and profit, in excessive desire for success or promotion, or in greed for possessions.

Equally we may find that our lack of happiness, our depression, is connected with the conditional happiness drive, in believing we can find lasting joy and pleasure in attachment. Attachment in this context means liking what is based on our own gratification from possessing (the word is purposely chosen) a good-looking boy/girl friend, clever children, expensive home; these not being loved for themselves, but for the glory we feel they reflect on us.

So what happens when the lover leaves us, the bright kids turn into surly drug-addicted teenagers, or we cannot meet the mortgage payments? These phenomena clearly represent another head of the Hydra. What can we do?

The failure of happiness makes us susceptible to negative emotions, that is to say, ones which drain our capacity for recognising our inter-being with others and all that this implies for love, care, awareness, and creative co-operation. Chief among these feelings are gloom, self-pity, guilt, irritation, hatred and anger (as opposed to outrage at cruelty or injustice). All of these naturally derive from and/or contribute towards ego-centricity. This is basically a failure to recognise the other as *real*, and hence to live in a world empty of the comfort fellow creatures could bring.

This condition of isolation and withdrawal is not only miserably unhappy, but one which by its very nature opens us wide to the Hydra forces.

But only when we begin to realise what is happening to us and to understand why, however dimly, can we take the first step towards a source of help. Otherwise we could dig ourselves a deeper pit of misery or fall prey to a sense of guilt that we may try to escape by the sad alternative of projecting the blame onto others.

In the second paragraph of this chapter, I observed that there were three things we should do. We have been discussing the first two, psychological, ones. The third was to share our understanding of the Hydra and its workings. We have already discussed how the generation of widespread feeling (the extended mind) brought about unexpected changes in South Africa; also in Eastern Europe in 1989 where the conventional wisdom had held that a virtually unarmed revolt, however ardent, could never topple states supported by well-armed troops.

I believe that although psycho-therapy and other healing skills may help us personally to overcome the Hydra's venom, nothing could match the power of comrades working together with a single mind (significant phrase). The centrepiece of my strategy, therefore, for taming the Hydra and stimulating happiness, is simply (simply? Yes, if we are sufficiently ardent) to save humanity's *joie de vivre* and indeed humanity itself, by meeting and talking. Talking and meeting in every possible context and drawing in every possible group and individual until an irresistible force of mind disarms the Hydra within ourselves and hence our institutions. And of course in the process, bit by bit, restructures society.

It all depends on the strength of our will and the collective strength of our will depends on our enlightening each other on the nature of our problem, which is the nature of the Hydra.

As the momentum increases it will be seen necessary to develop many new types of enterprise to repair the damage done by the Hydra and to fill gaps left by its heartlessly pragmatic view of human needs and rights.

I would expect that much of this would be educational because its essence should be the 'leading out' of potential rather than 'shoving it in'. It is to be expected that the chief foci for any education would be to examine and identify the most negative aspects of the global interdependency; to study and so far as possible to alleviate the pains of alienation; to study and *practise* the building of a network of positively peaceful relations; to *explore* relevant and creative approaches and suitable institutional frameworks for these activities.

In these and all other efforts it must be constantly stressed that the task of taming the Hydra, transforming the culture of violence and releasing happiness starts and indeed continues with trying to make these changes in ourselves. However, *this should never be separated from working on the ills of the world* – I do not mean by this that we should necessarily sally forth like crusaders or missionaries to benighted regions to deal with the dragons of war or tyranny, or to convert everyone who disagrees with us. On the contrary, we would often do better to stay put and tackle the source of alienation in our hearts, minds and homes, and to build up defences against the great illusions that underpin the Hydra. These are (1) that wealth equates health, (2) that peace can be bought by violence, (3) that ignorance is bliss, and (4) that happiness is for sale. And we must learn to mind our own business while remembering that, paradoxically, it is also everyone's business – and that everyone's is ours. For the forgetfulness, the lack of mindfulness and the deluded aspirations that animate the Hydra are born in the human heart.

Only when a critical mass of human beings have become attuned to this reality, can the current situation be significantly changed; we may then hope for a transformed Hydra no longer based on the fallacies of violence; and for a culture of nonviolent interdependence ignited by happiness.

Below the dank uncertainty
of an already rusted future,
the cringing fear, the panic button
no one ever answers;
below the crumbled dissolution
that denies our last poor hope,
abides the *All*, the unknown
splendid everlasting emptiness
whose glowing radiance pervades
all our realm unseen;
but minds unfocused only sense
a darkness lit with lurid flashes
of extinction.

Postscript

A personal message to the reader of the preceding instruction manual

Having, we hope, carefully studied the preceding pages, you are now in a position to take proud possession of your superb piece of equipment, your own PERSONALISED LIFE MACHINE (PLM). Good luck and Good Living.

You may at first, however, have a few little problems in actually *using* and *getting the best out of your PLM.* Perhaps when you first owned a car or a computer there were some minor problems. We therefore append a list of common difficulties, questions or malfunctions and how to deal with them:

You wonder if your PLM needs maintenance. Yes, daily and indeed constantly by yourself, and every so often by an expert.

You say your PLM doesn't go very well. Too bad, but you are the driver; perhaps you should take a course in mechanics or whatever you consider to be the appropriate skill.

You wonder if everyone really has the innate abilities to use it properly – some don't seem to. They really do, but these show in different ways and they may not develop for a very long time.

You don't understand how we can know this. By observation. If we treat people *as if* they were skilful or for that matter stupid, then smarter, or dumber, will they become.

You ask if this means we can change people. We are changing people and being changed by people all the time. We are all the products of each other's genes, acts, or thoughts; because all these influences are different, we are also all different.

You feel the local supermarket is hydratic but difficult to do without. Patronise the local corner shop, it may be more expensive, but you can buy less. You could of course blow up or burn down the supermarket, but that would be a hydratic solution to a hydratic problem.

You would like to give up your car, but are too strongly addicted to it. Sell it to the local scrap merchant and use the proceeds to give your family a treat; that will make you all feel better.

You feel miserable. Go and find someone more miserable than you are and tell them that their PLM is a great source of happiness; they should make use of it. (And so should you.)

You are worried about your investments. Get rid of them then; they won't be offended.

You are worried about keeping up your lifestyle. You are lucky to have a style to keep up. We suggest you keep it down instead.

You are worried about the state of the world and would like to do something to help but don't know what. You obviously are not worried enough; with any luck you'll find something worse which will worry you into action.

You are worried about ... Enough of this; all you need worry about is worrying.

You have found a new teacher who you think will save the world. He or she won't unless you do too, so get cracking.

You are afraid you may be too attached to your boy/girl friend. Don't worry, you will soon find out.

You are so upset you feel you could cut your throat. Better yours than someone else's, but better still to do something useful, like mending hurts rather than inflicting them.

You say you also don't understand the Hydra and what have the Greeks to do with it anyway? Nothing; as for the Hydra I don't suppose it understands you either. But don't bother about the word, it's just a fancy name for the violent and cruel things in the world, most of which are somehow connected by their shared greed and avarice.

You don't understand the extended mind. Nor do I; but I have experienced something to which I have applied that name.

You ask if the Hydra is a feature of the extended mind. I think it may be; someone cleverer than me needs to write a book about it.

You ask if other people should be allowed to use your PLM. Of course. If you don't, you will find it goes wrong very quickly.

IF YOU HAVE ANY FURTHER QUERIES OR COMPLAINTS YOU MAY REACH ME BY E-MAIL; fellowtraveller@demonic.conman.glob

Notes and bibliography

I need hardly say that what you have been reading is not an academic work. It is not based on meticulous study of research findings, nor is it presented in a scholarly fashion. My principal sources are the events through which I have lived and so have experienced either directly, or through my friends and colleagues, and obviously the media. Of course some reporting is inaccurate, limited or biassed; there are often at least two sides to a story, which makes evaluation difficult. On the whole, however, I respect the reporters who have written about the events I have been involved with. In any case, with the passing of time, the truth tends to become clear.

I have done my best to be detached and analytical in my assessments. In fact for twenty-eight years of my life I held university positions which facilitated scholarly study and reflection. For a somewhat shorter period, however, I have not had the advantage of a comfortable chair, but have instead had ample opportunity for thought and for carrying out my own enquiries unfettered by the ruthless cycle of university committees.

I have of course greatly profited from some academic writings, for example those of Elise and Kenneth Boulding, John Burton, Roger Fisher, John Paul Lederach, Scilla Elworthy, Paul Rogers, Christopher Mitchell, Christian Scherrer, Cynthia Sampson, Hugh Miall, Tom Woodhouse, Hizkias Assefa, Steve and Sue Williams, Simon Fisher among others.

I am bound to say, however, that I find most scholarly writing on conflict, peace, violence and the related topics of development (or more usually de-development) both tedious and lacking insight. The usual reason for this is that the people concerned have often never experienced what they are writing about. One needs to have lived through and to share the terror, confusion and desperation of war and other aspects of extreme violence to understand how and why some things happen. But for anyone lacking the imaginative genius of a great poet, to write about such things at second hand would be like the blind discussing colour or the deaf discussing sound.

In the 1970s very few academics shared my interest in peacemaking and mediation. Diplomats and politicians were, of course, involved in these things professionally. Also involved were members of various peace groups, such as

CND and the Peace Pledge Union, but their particular concern was protest, propaganda and demonstration. These are indeed important parts of the process, but more is also needed.

After a few years a more systematic approach developed; mediation became all the rage, a sort of universal panacea; booklets appeared offering fatuous simplifications of the whole process. (So did long, serious and – to me – unreadable books which had nothing to do with real life and feelings.) This popularity was worse than the earlier neglect; it promoted a series of gimmicky techniques that ignored the subtle, delicate, dangerous, tedious travail, possibly lasting many years, of coping with violence. (I should make it clear that I am talking of peacemaking in situations of large-scale sustained violence, actual or potential. Less complex, violent or emotionally fraught situations are sometimes more susceptible to routine treatment such as may be practised in schools or communities.)

Consequently I do not intend to justify statements or opinions (except in a couple of cases) with specific references (anyway, it has always seemed to me a bizarre convention that one can legitimise any absurd statement by quoting someone else who had the same silly idea). Instead, however, I shall mention readings that I have found particularly helpful in shaping my *Weltanschauung*.

My understanding of how things happen, their inter-relatedness, and the destructive cycles to which ignorance may lead, has been greatly increased by Buddhism, particularly of the Tibetan Vajrayana, through personal contact with His Holiness the Dalai Lama and the late Lama Yeshe. Buddhism is not so much a religion, being non-credal and agnostic, as a psychological philosophy. Of the Dalai Lama's many books I might suggest *The Good Heart*, Rider, London, 1993 and, because of its relevance to these pages, written with psychiatrist Howard C. Cutler, *The Art of Happiness: a handbook for living*, Hodder and Stoughton, London, 1988; Lama Yeshe's *Introduction to Tantra: Vision of Totality,* Wisdom Publications, London 1987, affected me greatly. Stephen Batchelor's *Buddhism Without Beliefs* presents Buddhism as a social and psychological teaching, not as a belief system. In a comparable category is Thomas Yeomans' *Soul Wound and Psychotherapy*, The Concord Institute, Pamphlet Series No 2, 1994.

Like all students of global development and underdevelopment, I am indebted to Ruth Leger Sivard's wonderful annual report on *Military and Social Expenditure*, World Priorities Link, Washington DC, USA, and to the periodical reports of organisations such as a joint publication of Earthscan with Safer World, *The True Cost Of Conflict*, London 1994; also the reports of

Oxfam, and the World Watch Institute. The recent publication of *The Mozambican Peace Project in Perspective* in *Accord*, a publication of Conciliation Resources, London, 1998, is an excellent example of accurate recording and analysis.

One book I read at school 65 years ago has remained in and fertilised my mind ever since – R.H. Tawney's *Religion and the Rise of Capitalism*, Faber, London, 1923. So has Edward Gibbon's *Decline and Fall of the Roman Empire*. This has many lessons for us, as in modern times does Jeremy Seabrook's *Victim of Development,* Verso, London and New York, 1993; both illustrate the workings of the Hydra. Seabrook's work shows in particular (like Dervla Murphy's *Ukinwe Road,* London, John Murray, 1995) how the best intentioned international agencies can play the same destructive part. What Seabrook does for the poor countries John Gray in *False Dawn: The Delusion of Global Capitalism,* Granta Books, London, 1998 does for the rich ones.

The chapter 'Mind, system and society' seeks to identify scientific explanations for phenomena with which I am acquainted, but through experience rather than by experiment. The work of Ilya Prigogine and Isabel Strengers, *Order out of Chaos*, Bantam Books, New York, 1984, and of Humberto Maturana and Francisco Varena, *The Tree of Knowledge*, Boston, Shambala, 1987 are consistent with my own untutored intuitions. So is that of Gregory Bateson in, for example, *Steps to an Ecology of Mind,* New York, 1972. James Lovelock's *Gaia,* Oxford University Press, 1979, widens the concept of mind to the planet, while Ken Wilber, among psychologists, extends the concept of mind/consciousness to levels beyond the individual. I have been guided through this maze of neurobiology, psychology and philosophy by Fritjof Capra, especially in *The Web of Life*, HarperCollins, London 1996.

Another entry into the realm of extended mind is the neglected, perhaps because sometimes popular (!) work of Lyall Watson. In *Lifetide: A biology of the unconscious*, London, Hodder and Stoughton, 1980, he tells, among other interesting things, the story of the 'Hundredth Monkey', which I refer to. I quote his references for this: M. Kawai, 'Newly acquired precultural behaviour of the natural troop of Japanese monkeys on Koshima Island', *Primates 6: 1-24,* 1965; and S. Kawamura, 'The process of subcultural propagation among Japanese monkeys' in C.B. Southwick, *Primate Social Behaviour,* Nostrand, Princeton, 1963.

Education is an underlying theme of many of the book's arguments.

A detailed master work in the field has been prepared by the Swedish Council of Churches: *Empowerment for Peace Service, A Curriculum for Education and Training for Violence Prevention, Nonviolent Conflict and Peace Building* for specific application in Croatia. The work has been initiated, co-ordinated and all but one chapter written by Margareta Ingelstam.

On issues of the traumatic impact of violence, both committed and suffered, I am impressed by *From Pain to Violence: the traumatic roots of destructiveness,* London, Whurr, 1993, by Felicity de Zulueta; the title alone could be a summary of what I have come to believe. Violence and its impact have been a thread running through the whole history of our times, so clearly presented by Eric Hobsbawm's *Age of Extremes*, Michael Joseph, London, 1994.

There are – good fruit from a ghastly tree – many fine books about the recent wars in Croatia and Bosnia. Of all I have read the most generally useful is perhaps *The Death of Yugoslavia*, Penguin Books & BBC Books, London, 1995, by Laura Silber and Allan Little.

I should mention that this short book is a companion volume to my *Another Way: Positive Response to Contemporary Violence,* Jon Carpenter, Oxford, 1995. For this reason some of the books referred to here also feature in its bibliography.

Finally, last and by no means least I recommend a book written by Michael Jacobs on behalf and representing the views of over 40 of the major British aid agencies, the Real World Cooperative, *The Politics of the Real World*, London, Earthscan, 1996.

Index

Adam Curle 1-2
Adam Curle's mother, religious atheist 87
Africa 13, 77
Asia 31
America, Civil War 13
Angola and Ethiopia, proxy wars 23
Arctic 23
Aristotle 35, 38
awareness 35, 86-87

Balkans 12
Bateson, Gregory on Mind 52-3
Belfast 82
Biafra 74
Blair, Tony 10
Bosnia 5, 23, 68, 77
Brecht, Berthold 38
Buddhism 8, 33, 40

Cambodia 77
Cambridge, MA 57
Caucasus 4, 13, 77
Chakmas, destruction of 4, 13, 47
Chile 33
China 12
Christianity 40
Churchill, Winston Spencer 57
Civil Resettlement Units 67-68
Clinton, Bill 10
Cold War, provokes violence 4, 16, 26
Colombia 4, 33
Croatia 68
counselling 67-68
culture of violence 5

Dalai Lama, HH the XIVth 38, 58
development, social rather than economic 31-33
  of ourselves 33-35
Diana, Princess, death 58
dissipative systems, Prigogine 51-53
Drumcree, point of tension in Northern Ireland 81

Eastern European nations liberation from Communist regimes 23, 56
education in post-war Japan and Germany 61-62
ego and awareness 88-89
emergence of the state 13-14
Ethiopia 4
Europe 23, 56
extended mind and awareness 55-59, 83

feed-back loops 54-55
Freud Sigmund, 52

Gaia 53, 57
Gandhi, M.K. 66, 87, *see* Satyagraha *and* Truth Force
Geneva 13
globalisation, unpredictability and variability 9-10, 79
Goya, F.J. 4
Great Lakes region of Africa 34
Greater Serbia 34
Guernica, painting by Pablo Picasso 4
Gulf War 27
Guatemala 4
G7P, the seven industrial plus other rich states 12, 15, 27-28, 79

happiness 37-49
  often deluded quest for 5
  as a natural drive 37-38
  source of 39-40
  religious approaches to 40
  primal 41
  existential 41-42
  conditional 42-43
  hazards to from desire 42
  externality and identity, threats to

happiness 40-45
illusion that wealth creates it 46-47
joie de vivre best describes it 48
necessary to tame the Hydra 79-81
Hitler, Adolf 52
Hinduism 49
Hydra, Greek mythological serpent, modern symbol 9-37
Hercules and the myth 9
and globalisation 9
'moral basis' of Pursuit and Protection (PPP) 10
European slave trade as early form of Hydra 11
origins of modern form 13-14
quasi-religious attitude to profit 19
our complicity in Hydra 19-20
Hydra to be transformed, not 'killed' 27
as a source of alienation 25
contributes to inequality 27-29
taming it 31-33
cause to fear it 57
summarising strengths and weaknesses 79-81
attracts those it most weakens 79

Indra's Net 46
International Monetary Fund 11,16, 27
interconnectedness and interdependency of forces comprising Hydra 13-17

Janata Vimukhti Peramuna (JVP) 4, 26, 27
Jesus 33
Jung, Karl Gustav 52

Kant, Immanuel 38
Keats, John 38
Kosovo 4
Kruhonja, Katarina 63-65

Lancaster House Conference (Zimbabwe) 75
Latin America 16, 31
Liberia 4

Maurana, Humberto 52
mediation 71-77
in Nigeria 74
Quakers and 74
in Zimbabwe 75
Robert Mugabe and 75
in Northern Ireland 75-76
in Sri Lanka 76-77
Miall, Hugh 56
Middle East 23
Milosevic, Slobodan 12
mind, studied by Bateson 52
its force generated by awareness 36
Mobutu, Sese Seko, former president of Zaire 54
Multinational Agreement on Investment, Hydra component 14
Muslims in Bosnian War 24

nineteen sixties, decade of change 56
Nkomo, Joshua, 25
North America 31
North Atlantic Treaty Organisation (NATO) 14-15
Northern Ireland 75
Norway 33
Nyerere, Julius, former president of Tanzania 75

Organiation for Economic Cooperation and Development (OECD) 15
Osijek Centre for Peace, Nonviolence and Human Rights 62-63

Pope, Alexander 30
Prigogine, Ilya 51-3
proxy wars, *see* Cold War *also* Angola, Ethiopia, South East Asia, etc. 23

Quakers, and mediation 71

Red Cross 68
remembering oneself, aid to awareness 67-68
resettlement 67-68
Russia 12, 15
Rwanda 4, 5, 24

Saddam Hussein, President of Iraq 10
Santayana, George 30
Satyagraha 66, *see also* Gandhi
Scandinavia 31

Serbs and Serbia 33
Sheldrake, Rupert 57
Sierra Leone 77
South Afrca 94
South East Asia 25
states, tendency for central control to disintegrate 5
strategy for happiness by reducing Hydra drive within ourselves; by recognising basic happiness; by sharing with others understanding of Hydra 85-91
strategy to tame the Hydra
  extend mind of nonviolence 87-88
  proaction by Osijek Centre 88-89
  Gandhian principles 89
Sukic, Krunoslav 63-65
systems 51-55

Tanzania 75
Teresa, Mother, 57-59
Terselic, Vesna 65
Tibet 4
Tiger Economies, essentialy vulnerable 11
torture, sub-culture of the culture of violence 17
training workshops 65-66
Tutsi 24

Uganda 5
UNHCR 68
United Kingdom 26, 28
United Nations 12, 14, 19, 26
USA 19, 22, 26
USSR 23, 33

violence, expansion after end of Cold War 4-5
violence and alienation 68-69

War 5
  changes in character and futility of 81
warlords, increasingly replace statesmen 5
Wijewira, Rohana, leader of JVP 74-75
Wilbur, Ken, psychologist 52
World Bank 11, 27
  favours Hydra globalisation 11
World War II 23, 67

Yugoslavia 4

Zaire 54
Zambia 75
Zimbabwe, liberation struggle 75
Zola, Emile 35

Also by Adam Curle

Another Way

Positive response to contemporary violence

This experienced international mediator draws on his first-hand experiences of violence and conflict in 35 countries (including most recently Sri Lanka and Bosnia) to analyse the crisis of violence that faces the world today.

His first-hand accounts of ongoing peace initiatives in Osijek and other places in former Yugoslavia are as relevant to social workers and teachers as to students of international politics and the inquiring lay reader.

Curle demonstrates that while violence is not itself new, the scale and the universality are very new, and this contemporary violence does not respond to conventional military, diplomatic or policing methods.

His model of a new approach to this violence is based on his experience of peace initiatives in the Croatian town of Osijek, where a small group is prevailing against an atmosphere of hatred, fear and militarism, in defiance of warlords and opposing factions.

A very moving and personal account of one man's attempt to help other people find peace.

"What is described here is the process of enabling both those of us who have done violence, and those to whom violence has been done, to transform our experience. This book is an essential piece of kit in the backpack of a blue helmet, in the briefcase of a diplomat, on the desk of a marriage guidance counsellor, or in the bunker of a warlord."
— from the Foreword by Scilla Elworthy, Oxford Research Group

"A fundamentally positive search for creative and effective ways to peace. Combines a lifetime of experience, study and reflection in seeking a response to contemporary violence." — Paul Rogers, Professor of Peace Studies, University of Bradford

"A succint historical, social scientific and philosophical explanation of the scope and roots of contemporary violence." — Kevin Clements, Director, Institute of Conflict Analysis and Resolution, George Mason University

"Points the way to step by step actions that can lead to healed communities in a healed world. Best of all he gives examples from violence-torn Croatia ... Opens the windows of mind and soul to the actual practice of making peace." — Elise Boulding, Professor Emerita of Sociology at Dartmouth College, President of the International Peace Research Association

£11.99 160pp, paperback ISBN 1 897766 22 X